Service and Service Systems

Service and Service Systems

Provider Challenges and Directions in Unsettled Times

Steve Baron, Philippa Hunter-Jones and
Gary Warnaby

businessexpert
Press

First published in 2014 by
Business Expert Press, LLC
222 East 46th Street, New York, NY 10017
www.businessexpertpress.com

ISBN-13: 978-1-60649-576-6 (paperback)
ISBN-13: 978-1-60649-577-3 (e-book)

Business Expert Press Service Systems and Innovations in Business and
Society Collection

Collection ISSN: 2326-2664 (print)
Collection ISSN: 2326-2699 (electronic)

Cover and interior design by Exeter Premedia Services Private Ltd.,
Chennai, India

First edition: 2014

10 9 8 7 6 5 4 3 2 1

Printed in the United States of America.

Abstract

Unsettled times can arise from a variety of causes, including environmental (e.g., earthquake), climatic (e.g., floods), economic (e.g., recession), social (e.g., illness), or political (e.g., civil unrest). They can result in citizens' loss of homes/possessions, jobs, health, or mobility. Citizens move from above the level of consumption adequacy, where their behaviors reflect long-term and higher-order needs, to below the level of consumption adequacy, where they are forced into a short-term focus on simple existence. In parallel, (service) organizations—utilities, transport, medical, cleaning, housing, education, broadcasting, national and local government—may become ineffective or unavailable: in other words, beyond the means of a significant proportion of citizens. This book explores the effect of unsettled times on spatial service systems. It provides original insights for managers of service organizations (especially public services), policy makers, and service system researchers and students.

Why Focus on Unsettled Times? Why Now?

The period 2009–2011 has witnessed multiple, high-profile, abnormal environmental and weather-related occurrences affecting citizens across the world; for example, wildfires in California, United States of America (2009), and Victoria, Australia (2009); "big freeze" in the United Kingdom (2009–2010); earthquake in Christchurch, New Zealand (2010); floods in Queensland, Australia (2010–2011). In Europe, austerity measures have resulted in mass unemployment. In Spain and Greece, youth unemployment is over 50%. Bird flu and influenza have affected Hong Kong and Thailand. War and civil unrest is ongoing in pockets of the Middle East. In all these cases, substantial numbers of citizens have fallen (temporarily) below the level of consumption adequacy, and service organizations have had to rethink their value propositions. Issues that are latent in settled times may become salient (albeit perhaps temporarily) in unsettled times. The identification of the salient issues is the challenge for the authors of the book, and one which we hope will inspire the readers to build upon with a view to the development of ongoing resilience within spatial service systems to better accommodate "shocks" to them during unsettled times.

Keywords

unsettled times, consumption adequacy, service systems, public services, places, spatial service systems

Contents

CHAPTER 1

Living in Unsettled Times

Defining and Characterizing "Unsettled Times"

In this book, we consider the impact of what we refer to as "unsettled times" on service systems. Service systems have been defined as "dynamic configurations of people, technologies, organizations and shared information that create and deliver value to customers, providers and other stakeholders."[1] Here we specifically focus on what could be termed *spatial* service systems; namely, where the boundaries of the system are defined primarily in terms of their geographical extent. Thus, towns, cities, regions, and—at an even broader spatial scale—even nations, could be thought of as service systems. Such spatial entities have been explicitly acknowledged as service systems.[2] These spatial service systems—and in particular, *urban* service systems—are our prime focus.

The next term requiring some explanation is "unsettled times." These can arise from a variety of causes which might impact on a specific spatial service system, including:

1. environmental (e.g., earthquake);
2. climatic (e.g., floods);
3. economic (e.g., recession);
4. social (e.g., illness); or
5. political (e.g., civil unrest).

Within the affected area, the result for citizens, of such unsettled times, could be loss of homes/possessions, jobs, health, or mobility. Citizens thus, could move from being above the level of consumption adequacy, to below the level of consumption adequacy. Here, we define consumption adequacy as the assumption that citizens have adequate resources to make choices of services (and products) that they consider for purchase, use, or both. When citizens fall below the level of consumption adequacy, they are forced into a short-term focus on simple existence.

In parallel to this, during periods of unsettled times, (service) organizations—public utilities, transport, medical, cleaning, housing, education, broadcasting, national, and local government—may become ineffective or unavailable: in other words, beyond the means of a significant proportion of citizens, for whatever reason. This book explores the effect of unsettled times on spatial service systems. It provides original insights for managers of service organizations (especially public services), policy makers, and service system researchers and students.

Living in Increasingly Unsettled Times?

In considering the above issues, a key question is, why focus on unsettled times, and why now?

The period 2009–2012 has witnessed multiple, high-profile, abnormal environmental and weather-related occurrences affecting citizens across the world: for example, wildfires in California, United States of America (2009), and Victoria, Australia (2009); the "big freeze" in the United Kingdom (2009–2010); earthquakes in Christchurch, New Zealand (2010–2011); floods in Queensland, Australia (2010–2011); super-storm Sandy in New York, United States of America (2012). Moreover, bird flu and influenza have affected Hong Kong and Thailand. War and civil unrest are ongoing in parts of the Middle East. Unsettled times can also be caused by other factors: in Europe, economic austerity measures have resulted in mass unemployment. In Spain and Greece, the majority of young people are unemployed. In all these cases, substantial numbers of citizens have fallen (albeit possibly only temporarily) below the level of consumption adequacy, and service organizations have had to rethink their value propositions. Issues that are latent in settled times may become salient in unsettled times. The identification of the salient issues is the challenge for this book, and one which we hope will inspire the readers to build upon with a view to designing spatial service systems to better accommodate "shocks" to them during unsettled times.

In this book, we will focus on unsettled times arising from environmental and climatic conditions. This is not to downplay the potential

impact of economic, social, and political factors, but the case studies arising from environmental and climatic conditions that we consider in this
book provide examples that better illustrate these issues for the purposes
of explanation.

The Need for Resilience

The extent to which such shocks can actually cause significant disruption to a system is, of course, relative. Taking weather for example, in
December 2012 parts of southern England had falls of 2 or 3 cm of snow,
which caused significant transport disruption, including the closure of
the runway at London Stansted Airport. One newspaper quotes an airline
passenger from Scandinavia:

> For us, this is crazy. A couple of inches of snow, which we would
> think nothing of in Finland, has caused so much chaos. They
> really should be better prepared to cope with problems like this.[3]

The above situation highlights the importance of system resilience—
namely, the abililty to anticipate, absorb, adapt to and/or recover from a
disruptive event[4]—to be able to cope with "shocks to the system." Thus,
taking this snow example, transport systems in Scandinavia, because of
generally more adverse climatic conditions in winter, need to be more resilient than those in the United Kingdom. However, all systems will inevitably be put under severe strain at some point in time as a consequence of
very extreme events or circumstances. It is this which we conceptualize as
"unsettled times," with potentially significant impact on the consumption
adequacy of those people reliant in some way upon a particular element of
an urban service system such as transport. These elements could, in turn,
be regarded as part of a "system of systems" (i.e., in this particular context,
the town or city as a whole, as discussed in Chapter 4). The concept of a
system of systems could be thought of as a collection of task-oriented or
dedicated systems that pool resources/capabilities to create a new, holistic,
more complex system offering greater functionality/performance.

   In designing urban service systems, when considering resilience in
order to develop a system that is proportionate to the risks involved, two

key issues arguably need to be explained—relative *impact* and relative *likelihood* of occurrence, which are considered in more detail below.

Impact

This could be conceptualized in terms of its scope, which could be thought of in spatial, functional, and temporal terms:

1. *Spatial* scope refers to the extent of the geographical area within which the impact of the event is felt, and also the extent to which this spatial extent is in some way discrete (in other words, the extent to which it corresponds—or not as the case may be—to administrative/governmental jurisdictional areas).

2. *Functional* scope relates back to the notion of a "system of systems." Thus, is the impact of the event confined to a particular part of an urban service system (such as transportation) or is the impact felt across the whole system? This also highlights the interconnectedness of urban service systems, as an adverse event impacting on one particular part of the urban service system could have much wider ramifications because of what could be termed the "ripple effect." The extent to which an event is containable to the particular part of the system from which it originates could, therefore, have a major influence on its ultimate impact.

3. *Temporal* scope relates to the length of time the impact is felt on the system. This will be a function of the nature of the disruptive event. Some events might have a major impact but only for a limited time period, whereas other events might be periodic in that they are most likely—although by no means certain—to occur at certain times (such as the "hurricane season" in the Caribbean and Gulf of Mexico). In contrast, the impact of other events may be ongoing. This links to the other key issue of relative likelihood.

Likelihood

This relates to the probability of occurrence of the shock to the system, and the consequent ability of the service system to anticipate and cope. It can be conceptualized in terms of two dimensions—propensity and preparedness.

As noted above, there may be some shocks that are potentially foreseeable because of a higher propensity of occurrence. For example, some disruptive events that are climatic in their origin can be characterized by inherent seasonality. Here, the likelihood of occurrence is increased at certain times of the year, and so those responsible for system design could build in an enhanced level of anticipation/preparedness during this period. With other events, a greater propensity for occurrence may be related to geography rather than time. For example, the pattern of earthquake zones on the planet is connected with the location of its tectonic plates. Thus, understanding the inherent risk associated with a disruptive event will inform the design parameters for an urban service system.

Theoretical Perspectives

This section briefly outlines the theoretical perspectives relating to research into service(s) from which we view the issues of service systems in unsettled times.

There is a 50-year history of research on service(s) marketing and management that has been driven by practical issues of the time.[5] The rationale for much of the research over the period has been on how, through improved service, organizations could achieve goals relating to financial gain (profitability; share of wallet), customer loyalty and patronage, competitive advantage, and positive word of mouth. Mechanisms for achieving these goals include increased customer satisfaction/delight, coupled with strategies associated with service quality, service recovery, and service employee development. While these goals and mechanisms still apply, this organizational perspective is increasingly thought to be limiting in the second decade of the 21st century, in which information and communication technology is a catalyst for changing citizen roles and activities in the context of a global economy.

Four streams of research have guided the focus of this book:

1. Service science
2. Service-dominant logic (SDL) of marketing
3. Transformative service research
4. Consumption adequacy

They are briefly introduced here, and are considered in more detail in Chapters 2 and 3.

Service Science

Service science is the study of service systems.[6] A prime focus of existing studies of service systems relates to how they are configured to enable and facilitate value co-creation (however defined). The individual is taken to be the smallest service system, with the global economy as the largest. The focus in this book is on urban places (and the communities therein) as service systems, and on the efficiency, effectiveness, and sustainability of such systems. Service science is supported by insights from the SDL of marketing.

Service-Dominant Logic of Marketing

Since it was first proposed by Vargo and Lusch,[7] the SDL of marketing has had a pronounced effect on research in marketing, service, and management. It is presented as a mindset governed by 10 foundational premises. Instead of regarding services (plural) as outcomes, the SDL is underpinned by service (singular) which is defined as "the application of skills and knowledge for the benefit of another party."[8] The SDL opens up the opportunity to examine resources of all "actors" in a system, and value co-creation activities which are not limited to firms/organizations.

Transformative Service Research

Under the banner of transformative service research, the firm-related goals of financial gain and service improvement outlined above are being supplemented by goals which represent more directly the citizen perspective: quality of life and citizen well-being. Viewing goals from a citizen perspective, together with an increased focus on consumer roles in service, provides a distinctive underpinning for the approach adopted in the book.

Consumption Adequacy

In almost all cases, service(s) marketing and management research has made the assumption that consumers have adequate resources to make choices of services (and products) that they consider for purchase. The concept of consumption adequacy makes clear that this is not the case for a large proportion of the world's citizens. People who lie above the level of consumption adequacy "can rise above a short-term focus on continued existence and are able to concentrate on consumption behaviors associated with long-term and higher-order needs."[9] Those who lie below it, cannot. In this book we focus on those who move from above, to below (albeit possibly only temporarily), the level of consumption adequacy during "unsettled times."

Readership and Aims

The book is written for final year marketing and management undergraduate students, MBA students, and business professionals who desire to understand established and innovative service research findings and their relevance to practice. The specific aims are:

1. to bring attention to the challenges of providing service to citizens below the level of consumption adequacy in unsettled times;
2. to apply research findings from service science, SDL of marketing, transformative service research, and consumption adequacy to meet these challenges;
3. to provide a practically useful classification of unsettled times;
4. to highlight the interactions and networks of "actors" that have salience in unsettled times;
5. to offer context through examples and a detailed case study;
6. to identify the implications for service organizations, policy makers, and service science research.

We hope that, by presenting the provider challenges in an engaging way, we can stimulate co-created solutions to deal with this increasingly complex situation.

Structure of the Book

The book is organized as follows:

In Chapter 2, we introduce in more detail the theoretical perspectives of service science, the SDL of marketing, and transformative service research that inform the content of the rest of the book.

As noted above, the main focus of this book is on unsettled times and their implications in relation to consumption adequacy of those individuals living through such times. Chapter 3 briefly outlines the concept of consumption adequacy, in the specific context of urban places as the stress caused by the massive growth of urban conurbations (especially in the developing world) places severe strain on urban service systems in these cities, with the result that the impact of "unsettled times" is potentially more likely to be significant and harmful.

Chapter 4 considers in more detail the notion of an urban service system, informed by service science concepts. It introduces the different elements of service systems—people, organizations, shared information, and technology—and analyzes their applicability in the specific context of cities as service systems, with particular emphasis on those issues relating to quality of life.

Chapter 5 introduces us to three instances of unsettled times—floods in Queensland, Australia (2010–2011), earthquake and tsunami in Japan (2011), and earthquakes in Christchurch, New Zealand (2010–2011)—highlighting the implications for the service systems in the places concerned.

Chapter 6 uses the three case studies outlined in Chapter 5 to conceptualize and classify the notion of unsettled times in more detail. It explores the similarities and differences in service system responses drawing on the dimensions of impact and likelihood briefly introduced above.

These issues are considered in more detail in relation to one specific instance in Chapter 7. Here, we consider the "big freeze" in the United Kingdom in 2010.

As with the case studies in the previous chapter, we use newspaper reports as source material. These newspaper reports are drawn from two particular datasets: the "United Kingdom Nationals" group; and the "UK Newspaper Stories" group. The United Kingdom Nationals group is a source of data which contains the full-text material of 16 national newspapers distributed throughout the United Kingdom. The UK Newspaper Stories group contains the content of all newspapers published in the United Kingdom which are carried on LexisNexis, a corporation providing technology-assisted legal research services. Typically all the newspapers included in both datasets cover a range of both national and international news stories in depth.

In Chapter 8, we reflect on the lessons learned through the focus on periods of "unsettled times." A number of purposeful proposals are made which build on the resulting insights, and which provide directions for innovative research. Implications for practice and policy are outlined, especially with regard to a suggested classification of unsettled times, and novel ways of considering citizens' resources and roles. The topic and research are in their infancy, and so we finish with an invitation for interested readers to join in with research based on the ideas put forward in the book.

Review and Discussion Questions

1. Define the following terms as used in the chapter: unsettled times; consumption adequacy; service systems; impact; likelihood.
2. Briefly explain the fundamentals of: service science; service-dominant logic; transformative service research.
3. How would you explain the difference between customers, consumers, citizens and stakeholders?
4. Give examples of unsettled times brought about through political, social or economic changes to a region.
5. What do you see as the main differences between customer satisfaction and citizen quality of life?

CHAPTER 2

Schools of Thought

Introduction

The four streams of research underpinning the insights in the book were identified in the previous chapter as:

1. service science;
2. service-dominant logic (SDL) of marketing;
3. transformative service research (TSR); and
4. consumption adequacy.

The first three streams represent current schools of thought emanating from the service research literature, and will be discussed in this chapter. The fourth stream, consumption adequacy, a fundamental concept of life experience and quality of life, will be dealt with in more detail in Chapter 3.

From a service research perspective, service in "unsettled times" has been a neglected area of study despite the variety of causes of—and seemingly increasing frequency of occurrence of—unsettled times outlined in the Introduction. However, the need for such a focus has been clearly identified by proponents of both service science and the SDL. Lusch and Spohrer maintain that:

> It is more important than ever to pay special attention to service system resiliency and sustainability. The emergence and growth of service science and service-dominant logic helps to encourage systems-level thinking and provides at least some initial guidance on developing appropriate 'mind-sets' and skills. In turn, this provides the means to be more innovative in developing solutions to 'wicked' human problems that growing complexity brings forth.[1]

The service science and SDL schools of thought have each emerged over the previous decade, and have much in common, as the quote above suggests. The study of service systems (service science) has been enabled through the use of language, perspectives, and assumptions adopted in SDL.[2] The origins of service science and SDL are different and so we treat them in separate sections, notwithstanding their subsequent convergence.

Service Science

Maglio and Spohrer define service science as the study of service systems, with the aim of enabling systematic service innovation.[3] Service science is a practitioner-initiated response to the global demand for more knowledge-intensive and customized service which acknowledges the participation of the multitude of actors involved in service innovation. Service systems are:

> value-co-creation configurations of people, technology, value propositions connecting internal and external service systems, and shared information (e.g., language, laws, measures, and methods).[4]

In 2009, a journal, *Service Science*, was launched to encourage "state-of-the-art research and development in the service science and related research, education and practice areas."[5] A specific purpose of the journal is to act as a forum for *both academicians and practitioners*, and it has a main focus on *people's* satisfaction. Human problems are fundamental to the study of service science.

What is of particular relevance to the topic of this book is that the city, as a service system, has attracted the attention of service science advocates, especially those employed by IBM. Given that many causes of unsettled times (e.g., environmental, climatic, economic, social, or political) affect specific geographical regions, insights on cities as service systems are especially helpful as over half the world's population is urban rather than rural, which can cause numerous problems (as discussed in the next chapter). Service science offers a transdisciplinary approach to cities as service systems, and, as such, identifies systems, stakeholders, and resources that are integral to a city.

There are systems that:

1. focus on the *flow of things* (transport and supply chains; water and waste; food and products; energy and electricity; information and communication technology);
2. support people's *activities* (building and construction; retail and hospitality; banking and finance; healthcare and family; education and work);
3. focus on *human governance* (at city, state, and nation levels).

Stakeholders include customers, providers, authorities, and competitors, while resources include people, technology, information, and organizations.[6]

Key to the study of cities as service systems is the recognition of the *interconnectedness* of the sub-systems, stakeholders, and resources, and the focus on the well-being of citizens. Dirks et al. observe that "Quality of life and the attractiveness of a city are profoundly influenced by the core systems of a city: transport, government services and education, public safety and health."[7] The core systems clearly do not work independently. For example, for health and education services to work efficiently and effectively, teachers, pupils, doctors, nurses, and patients all rely on transport services and infrastructures to meet their daily obligations. In a city, or other geographical regions, there are complex networks of interactions between the systems, stakeholders, and resources identified in the previous paragraphs. In settled times, they are often overlooked, latent, and taken for granted. In unsettled times, they become salient, and this provides a lens to understand more clearly the human problems brought about by their complexity, and offer innovative solutions. The case study of the United Kingdom's "big freeze" (outlined in Chapter 7) provides some specific examples of these phenomena.

Service-Dominant Logic

The SDL, according to Vargo and Akaka is offered as "a service-centered alternative to the traditional goods-centered paradigm for understanding economic change and value creation that has been identified as an appropriate philosophical foundation for the development of service science."[8] It is based on the notion that service, which is defined, according to Vargo and Lusch, as "the application of skills and knowledge for the benefit of another party"[9] is the fundamental unit of exchange. In the context of marketing, it offers a unifying theory which embraces the previously separate sub-disciplines of goods and services marketing, and includes both business-to-business (B2B) and business-to-consumer (B2C) marketing. However, it has a wider influence than the discipline of marketing. It has potential for providing a lens for a greater understanding of markets and society.[10]

The SDL is underpinned by 10 foundational premises (FPs) (shown in Table 2.1 below). Before looking at the FPs in more detail, it is worth pointing out why it has become such a challenge to the marketing orthodoxy that preceded it.

Historically, marketing had a focus on physical goods, as many economies were manufacturing-led. In the late 1960s and early 1970s, as services were becoming a greater proportion of nations' GDP, services marketing began to grow as a separate sub-discipline. Services, like goods, were seen as (economic) outputs, whose values were determined by the provider. This approach has been retrospectively labeled as the goods-dominant logic (GDL) of marketing, to contrast it with the SDL approach. SDL offers a different mindset through which to view value and interactions. As seen above, it is based on service (singular) as a process, rather than services (plural) as an output, with goods, when involved, being seen as vehicles for service provision.[11] According to SDL, providers do not create value, and can only offer value propositions. Value is co-created between "actors" in a service system. There is an emphasis on the importance of the use and integration of operant resources (the intangible resources that produce effects) by all parties (including individual customers/citizens) in value co-creation processes. This contrasts with a focus on operand resources; those resources which must be acted on to be beneficial, such as natural resources, goods, and other generally static matter.[12] Table 2.1 provides the 10 FPs.[13]

Table 2.1. Service-Dominant Logic: The 10 Foundational Premises[14]

Number	Foundational Premise (FP)
FP1	*Service is the fundamental basis of exchange* The SDL is based on the notion that service is exchanged for service. Service is the application of specialized competences (operant resources—knowledge and skills) through deeds, processes, and performances, for the benefit of another entity or the entity itself. Goods and services are not alternative forms of products. Goods, when employed, are aids to the service provision process.
FP2	*Indirect exchange masks the fundamental basis of exchange* Because service is provided through complex combinations of goods, money, and institutions, the service basis of exchange is not always apparent.
FP3	*Goods are a distribution mechanism for service provision* Goods (both durable and non-durable) derive their value through use—the service they provide. Goods are not regarded as units of output embedded with value, as in the goods-dominant logic.
FP4	*Operant resources are the fundamental source of competitive advantage* Knowledge and skills are examples of operant resources, and their application can generate a variety of competitive advantages.
FP5	*All economies are service economies* Service (singular) is only now becoming more apparent with increased specialization and outsourcing. Service reflects a process of using one's resources for the benefit of another entity.
FP6	*The customer is always a co-creator of value* Value creation is interactional. Consumers want to interact with firms to co-create value. Co-production is a component of co-creation of value when customers participate in the development of the core offering, for example, in mobile phone design.
FP7	*The enterprise cannot deliver value, but only offer value propositions* Enterprises can offer their applied resources for value creation, and collaboratively (interactively) create value following acceptance by users of value propositions, but cannot create, deliver, or both value independently. Value is "value-in-use."
FP8	*A service-centered view is inherently customer oriented and relational* Because service is defined in terms of customer-determined benefit, it is inherently customer oriented. Because value is co-created, it is inherently relational: value cannot be created any other way.
FP9	*All social and economic actors are resource integrators* The context of value creation is networks of networks (resource integrators). Individuals are resource integrators, including customers/consumers.
FP10	*Value is always uniquely and phenomenologically determined by the beneficiary* Value is idiosyncratic, experiential, contextual, and meaning-laden. Enterprises and customers can be both providers and beneficiaries. It emphasizes the importance of understanding customer experiences.

The key FPs for the topic of this book are FP1, FP6, FP7, FP9, and FP10, which provide very useful insights into how to interpret service systems in unsettled times:

1. By considering service (singular), as specified in FP1, it is possible to acknowledge everyday (non-remunerated) practices (such as caring for the family), as well as service offered by organizations to customers, all within the same logic.

2. F6, F7, and F10 make it clear that value is not solely created by organizations or enterprises, but must involve co-creation with customers/beneficiaries. Organizations can only offer value propositions. "Value-in-use" occurs when value is co-created with customers and determined by them.

3. FP9, with its emphasis on *all* social and economic actors, recognizes the resources—especially intangible ones—that customers are able to use and integrate. Prior to the 21st century, customer resources, especially intangible resources, such as knowledge and skills, did not receive anything like the attention that was given to organizational resources. The onset of social media opportunities and practices has brought customer skills, knowledge, imagination, and invention, together with customer-to-customer (C2C) interactions, to the forefront. SDL offers a solid platform for their consideration and understanding. Through SDL, customer/citizen resource inputs to service system resilience are made explicit.

Transformative Service Research

In the GDL, where value is determined by the provider, there has been a natural tendency to view service(s) from a provider perspective. Correspondingly, research has focused on fulfilling firm/organizational goals such as profitability and competitive advantage. The relatively recent research stream of TSR puts forward the case for a focus on promoting human well-being. Rosenbaum et al. contend that TSR "treats outcomes related to consumer well-being, including quality-of-life issues as important, managerially relevant, and worthy of study."[15] TSR has been defined as "the integration of consumer and service research that centers on creating uplifting changes and improvements in the well-being of consumer entities: individuals (consumers and employees), communities and the ecosystem."[16]

Studies of interactions between "service entities" and "consumer entities" within a macro environment, with well-being outcomes as the goal, provide a basic framework for engaging in TSR. Service entities are represented at macro and micro levels by sector (e.g., health), organization (e.g., a hospital), offering (e.g., antenatal care), process (e.g., home visits), and employee (e.g., midwife). Consumer entities also are considered at different levels: individual (e.g., patient), collective (e.g., family or community), and ecosystem (e.g., public health). The key macro environmental aspects providing a broader context for TSR research are public policy, cultural, technological and economic. For example, a policy prohibiting smoking in public places for public health reasons may be appreciated by some cultures more than others. A policy of filling in tax returns electronically may save costs but also make life difficult for some consumers. The interactions that are considered are within customer and service entities (e.g., interpersonal encounters) as well as between customer and service entities, as part of value co-creation processes. Readers are directed to Anderson et al. to follow the detailed arguments in favor of taking a TSR approach.[17]

The TSR approach does provide an insightful direction for current service research. The change in the research mindset is very noticeable. It is particularly important in shifting the focus away from the global minority of well-off consumers to a consideration of consumers who lack the resources and choices to increase their well-being and quality of life to levels often assumed by research that takes a firm/organization perspective to service(s). Contrast the TSR priorities, below in Table 2.2, with those in the late 1990s dealing with the concept of "customer delight." Then, there was a focus on "delighting the customer as an extension of providing basic satisfaction."[18] Service delight was offered as a strategy for businesses to attain profitability and competitive advantage. As Rust and Oliver contend: "Delighting the customer can be a profitable business practice."[19] Our research into unsettled times arising from environmental and climatic conditions (as reported in Chapters 5 and 7) suggests that, depending on circumstances, customer delight may mean something far more basic than a contrast with customers' raised expectations, even in advanced economies.

The TSR future research priorities in Table 2.2 have been identified through forums of international service researchers which have taken place in the second decade of the 21st century.

Table 2.2. Transformative Service Research Priorities[20]

Improving consumer and societal welfare through service;
Enhancing access, quality, and productivity in health care and education;
Delivering service in a sustainable manner;
Motivating the development and adoption of green technologies and related services;
Planning, building and managing service infrastructure for metropolitan areas, regions, and nations;
Democratizing public services for the benefit of consumers and society;
Driving service innovation at the base of the pyramid.
Ostrom et al.
Reducing, through service entities, the disparities in well-being experienced by poor consumers and ethnic minorities;
Focusing on the influence of value co-creation activities on consumer and employee well-being;
Strategies for increasing consumer willingness, and business and government engagement with sustainable service(s).
Anderson et al.

Such priorities fit, in general, with the intention, in later chapters, to focus on citizens experiencing unsettled times. The current TSR focus is on service sectors (financial services, health services, social services) and how they might be improved through the adoption of its framework and goals. Our issue in this book is on the resiliency of such services (and the service systems of which they are a part) to (unexpected) "shocks."

Summary

The focus on service in unsettled times is relevant to this day and age, in a world where everything seems much more interconnected. To provide a soundly based study, it has been extremely helpful to draw on insights, from the past 8 years or so, emanating from three inter-related schools of thought: service science, SDL, and TSR:

1. From service science, we are guided by a focus on service systems, especially those reflecting a geographical region such as a city, with citizen quality-of-life and innovations as priorities.

2. From SDL, we are guided by the underpinning concept of service (as opposed to services), the importance of co-creation of value between "actors" in a service system, and the attention given to customer use and integration of resources (in addition to organizational use and integration of resources).

3. From TSR, we are guided by the focus on customer/citizen well-being and the research directions that acknowledge the life experiences of the less fortunate consumers.

We finish this chapter with another quote from Lusch and Spohrer which provides further support for the purpose of this book:

> ...service quality researchers should both increase their study of citizens, as customer/stakeholder impacted by regional quality-of-life measures and the IT transformation of government and health-care service systems.[21]

In the following chapter, we introduce the fourth school of thought from which we draw the concept of consumption adequacy as a means of exploring quality of life experienced by less fortunate citizens.

Review and Discussion Questions

1. Explain the systems, stakeholders and resources that are integral to a city.

2. Discuss how value is co-created by "actors" in a service system.

3. Why is it considered important to view customers, as well as organizations, as resource integrators?

4. Explain, in your own words, the essential differences between the goods-dominant and service-dominant logics of marketing.

5. Examine the last 3 years' issues of the journal *Service Science*. What appear to be the current topics of interest?

CHAPTER 3

Consumption Adequacy

Introduction

This chapter focuses on the last of the four streams of thought that were identified in Chapter 1, namely, *consumption adequacy*.

While the other three schools of thought (described in more detail in the previous chapter) have a more overt focus on the *academic* concepts underpinning this book, this chapter will use theory as a framework to consider in more detail the specific *context* in which the impact of unsettled times is felt. We begin by discussing consumption adequacy within the context of the concept of the "bottom of the pyramid" (BoP). We then move on to describe the increasingly important *urban* context, recognizing that the majority of the world's population now live in an urban rather than a rural environment. Here, drawing on the notion of operant and operand resources (discussed in the context of the service-dominant logic [SDL] in Chapter 2), we focus on the notion of urban resources —and their allocation—to facilitate the development of spatial competitive advantage for urban places (recognizing that cities and towns are increasingly perceived as being in competition with each other—for inward investment, residents, tourist visitors, and so on), and also for the quality of life of urban residents. This leads to the notion of cities and towns as urban service systems—the operation and effectiveness of which may be adversely affected by "unsettled times"—which is developed in more detail in Chapter 4. However, we begin by setting the context for this by briefly considering consumption adequacy in an urban context.

The "Bottom of the Pyramid"

Any discussion about consumption adequacy should be contextualized by the concept of the "bottom of the pyramid" (BoP—sometimes referred to as "base of the pyramid"). This concept was originally introduced to draw attention to the 4–5 billion poor on the planet who are unserved or underserved by the large organized private sector, including multinational firms.[1] Drawing on the human development categories advanced by the United Nations, Martin and Hill emphasize the extent of different levels of global poverty, stating that:

> about three-fourths of the planet's population live in nations with less than ideal material conditions, defined by low levels of marketplace abundance and lack of bargaining power necessary to access this abundance.[2]

More specifically, Martin and Hill cite figures from 2007 that break down the world's population according to level of human development as follows:

1. Very High Human Development Countries   14.79% of total world population
2. High Human Development Countries   13.77% of total world population
3. Medium Human Development Countries   65.67% of total world population
4. Low Human Development Countries   5.77% of total world population

They contrast "the material landscape of too much" which characterizes the countrywide marketplace experience of those 15% of the world's consumers who exist at the very top of the pyramid with the experience of consumers in those nations comprising the bottom two levels of the pyramid which is "characterized by too little."[3] Of course, such figures can be regarded as a generalization—there will be consumers in very high human development countries who do not enjoy the concomitant benefits, and whose lives are characterized by severe deprivation. Indeed, Martin and Hill argue that a nuanced understanding is required, which recognizes the complexities of the interrelationships involved.

Summarizing lessons drawn from the debates about what constitutes the BoP, and taking an explicit management-oriented perspective that the BoP constitutes a business opportunity, Prahalad identifies five key issues:

1. These 4–5 billion consumers (and also producers) constituting the bottom levels of the pyramid represent a potentially very significant market and also can be regarded as an engine of innovation, vitality, and growth.

2. These consumers do not constitute a monolith and will represent extreme variety in an array of variables such as geographical mix, income levels, cultural and religious differences, and so forth. Consequently, the BoP can be likened to a kaleidoscope, where no single perspective illuminates the totality of the phenomenon.

3. The groups at the BoP can be segmented in various ways, and no institution needs to serve all of the BoP—Prahalad notes that serving the "next billion" is as legitimate as serving the "bottom billion."

4. Indeed, there is a segment that is so destitute and deprived, and subject to war and disease, and so forth (i.e., linked to the low human development countries mentioned above), that they need other forms of help (such as government subsidies, multilateral aid, and philanthropy of various kinds) in order to facilitate capacity building to enable them to escape poverty and deprivation through self-sustaining market-based systems.

5. Active engagement with the BoP requires new and innovative approaches to business.[4]

Emphasizing the need for a nuanced approach to understanding the BoP, given the fact that issues relating to life satisfaction, well-being, and poverty will vary significantly according to context, Martin and Hill suggest that the effect of BoP factors is subject to moderation, depending on the existence of a baseline of goods and services deemed necessary for survival—the concept of *consumption adequacy*, discussed in more detail below.

Consumption Adequacy

Hill defines consumption adequacy as:

> [T]he continuous availability of a bundle of goods and services that are necessary for survival as well as the attainment of basic human dignity and self-determination. This bundle contains subsistence products such as food, clothing, shelter, and healthcare. In addition, goods and services that provide or support education, training, and decent job opportunities that help people envision and achieve a better future are included.[5]

In other words, these goods and services are the ones that must be acquired before citizens within a particular nation "can rise above a short term focus on continued existence and are able to concentrate on consumption behaviors associated with long-term and higher order needs."[6] Hill emphasizes that the specific nature of those goods and services deemed "necessary" in this context will depend on prevailing community and cultural factors in the particular area in which consumers are embedded, but Martin and Hill suggest that consumption *inadequacy* is a composite of deprivations in relation to education, healthcare, and nutrition, as well as in key services such as water, sanitation, and electricity. Absence of such factors can have an obvious detrimental effect on, for example, perceived autonomy, self-determination, and life satisfaction of individuals.

Nussbaum suggests that a life worthy of human dignity at a bare minimum requires an ample threshold level of the following "central capabilities" (which is the task of the government to provide in order for its citizens to pursue a dignified and minimally flourishing life). The presence of these "central capabilities" provides a baseline that allows consumption adequacy to occur:

1. Life—Having a normal lifespan; not dying prematurely, or before life is so reduced so as to be not worth living
2. Bodily Health—Enjoying good health, with adequate nourishment and shelter

3. Bodily Integrity—Freedom of movement from place to place, to be secure against violent assault (including sexual assault and domestic violence) and having opportunities for sexual satisfaction and choice with regard to reproduction

4. Senses, Imagination, and Thought—Being able to use the senses in order to imagine, think, and reason in a truly human way, informed and cultivated by an adequate education, and also being able to practice artistic expression if desired

5. Emotions—Being able to have attachments to things and people outside ourselves, and not having one's emotional development blighted by fear and anxiety

6. Practical Reason—Being able to form a conception of the good and to engage in critical reflection about the planning of one's life

7. Affiliation—Relating to (1) Being able to live with and toward others, recognizing and showing concern for others and engaging in forms of social interaction, and being able to imagine the situation of another; and (2) Having the social bases of self-respect and non-humiliation; being treated as a dignified being whose worth is equal to others

8. Other Species—Being able to live with and concern for animals, plants, and the world of nature

9. Play—Being able to laugh, play, and enjoy recreational activities

10. Control Over One's Environment—In terms of (1) Political—being able to participate effectively in political choices and having the protection of free speech and association; and (2) Material—being able to hold property and having property rights on an equal basis with others, having the right to seek employment on an equal basis with others, and so on.[7]

The Urban Context

In a contemporary global environment, many of the issues relating to consumption adequacy in terms of the capabilities mentioned above are directly related to the urban context for much of the world's population. This is inevitable given the increasingly urbanized world in which we live.

Burdett and Rode note that while only 2% of the earth's surface is occupied by cities, they account for 53% of the world's population, a figure expected to grow to 75% by 2050.[8]

A key trend in urban development is the growth of the megacity, defined as urban agglomerations with 10 million inhabitants or more. Smith notes that from just two megacities in 1950 and three in 1975, their number increased to 19 by 2007, and there are expected to be 27 by 2025. Moreover, Smith emphasizes that in terms of sheer size alone, global urban culture is shifting eastwards—of the eight new megacities anticipated in the next 15 years, five are in Asia, three in Africa, and only one in Europe. In addition, population growth will also occur in urban agglomerations of all sizes—the number of "large" cities (i.e., with populations of between 5 and 10 million) is expected to rise from 30 in 2007 to 48 by 2025, with three quarters of these in developing countries. This urban growth in developing countries will be due to high birth rates and also by attracting migrants from rural areas, and indeed rural settlements will be transformed into urban regions. This has had a concomitant impact on rural populations. Smith notes that the world's rural population is expected to peak at around 3.5 billion in 2018 or 2019, and will then gradually fall to around 2.8 billion by 2050.[9]

Burdett and Rode state that the number of people classified as urban poor is rising. Notwithstanding this fact, urbanization has helped to reduce absolute poverty (given the fact that poverty levels in urban areas are generally lower than those in rural areas). Glaeser states that:

> [C]ities aren't full of poor people because cities make people poor, but because cities attract poor people with the prospect of improving their lot in life. The poverty rate among recent arrivals to big cities is higher than the poverty rate among long-term residents, which suggests that, over time, city dwellers' fortunes can improve considerably.[10]

However, it cannot be ignored that, overall, 33% of city dwellers live in slums, although this figure masks wide variances.[11] Davis defines a slum as being "characterized by overcrowding, poor or informal housing, inadequate access to safe water and sanitation, and insecurity of tenure"—in other words, manifesting many of the deficiencies relating to Nussbaum's "central capabilities" outlined above. Davis notes that whilst this definition was officially adopted at a United Nations meeting in October 2002, it is somewhat limited in that it:

> is "restricted to the physical and legal characteristics of the settlement", and eschews the more difficult-to-measure "social dimensions", although it equates under most circumstances to economic and social marginality.[12]

Davis suggests that there are probably more than 200,000 slums on the planet, ranging in population from a few hundred to over a million people.

Such urban growth has inevitable consequences across a whole range of aspects of human existence. Burdett and Rode note that growth has an environmental impact on a locality, which will most likely affect disadvantaged people disproportionately as they live in precarious structures in more vulnerable locations. As urban economies become more prosperous, the wider environmental impact—in terms of carbon emissions, energy, electricity and water consumption, dwelling and transport patterns, and so on—will also be felt.[13] Urban infrastructure—in both developed and developing regions—will therefore need to change and adapt to meet these changing conditions. Indeed, the ability of individual urban areas to accommodate these developments, in terms of their social—and, equally importantly, their economic—implications, will influence how an urban place is perceived in terms of the quality of life of those residing therein. This will also have significant implications for how urban resources (of all kinds) are integrated and used, which in turn, will impact on the perceived economic competitiveness of individual urban places in an increasingly globalized economy. Indeed, there is a substantial body of literature which considers urban competitiveness more generally. Drawing from this literature on urban competitiveness as context, the rest of this chapter will focus on the resources that urban places can use in order to develop and maintain as good a quality of life for its inhabitants as is possible.

Urban Resources

The configuration of resources that an urban area has at its disposal will influence the extent to which a particular urban place is regarded as being competitive in comparison with other cities and towns. Turok states that an important imperative for success in this regard is the creation of place distinctiveness: "the basic proposition is that, by developing specialized activities and strong creative capabilities, cities can build sources of competitive advantage that other places cannot readily reproduce." Sources of competitive advantage can include advanced knowledge/expertise (that are dynamic and enable continuous upgrading to higher value activities over time), whereas others are more intangible, associated with "quality" (which serve to limit the amount of direct competition with other places in terms of labor and property costs, extent of government subsidies etc.). The emphasis, Turok suggests, "is on being 'smarter' and creating products, services, and environments that cannot be copied"[14]—in other words, developing space-specific *resources* that are attractive to existing and potential place users.

Following on from this, Musterd and Murie identify four main theoretical frameworks that have been put forward to conceptualize the essential conditions for urban competitiveness in an increasingly globalized world.[15] These essential conditions can be thought of in terms of urban *resources*, and are outlined in more detail below.

"Hard" Conditions

First, the most established and well-known theoretical approach focuses on the creation of *"hard" conditions* that are attractive to investors, and so on. These would include, for example, availability of capital and an appropriately skilled labor force, an institutional context with the right set of regulations and sufficiently attractive tax regimes, good infrastructure and accessibility, availability, and affordability of office space, and increasingly important, educational facilities (particularly high-quality public schools and universities).

Economic Cluster Theory

The second approach—*economic cluster theory*—utilizes the concept of agglomeration, emphasizing that activities are assumed to cluster together in a particular place because they have linkages to each other, use the same public and private services and institutions, and are connected to the same environment, while profiting from each other's presence. Porter defines clusters as "geographic concentrations of interconnected companies and institutions in a particular field. Clusters encompass an array of linked industries and other entities important to competition."[16] This concept has had widespread influence in both the academic and policy arenas in terms of explaining spatial competitiveness.[17]

Network Theory

Musterd and Murie state that the differences between the hard conditions and cluster approaches in explaining urban competitiveness are relative rather than absolute, and suggest that many related debates might also be positioned under a third heading, namely, *network theory*. This approach focuses on the impact of personal ties, local relations, and organizational affiliations. The resonance with cluster theory is obvious, but this network approach is distinguished by a more overt focus on the concept of embeddedness. Here, a key issue relates to the motives influencing place stakeholders in their decisions about where to settle and where to stay, and this approach introduces a criterion for differentiation on the basis of the origins and history of an individual's personal relationships (e.g., place of family, place of birth, place of study, proximity to friends etc.).

"Soft" Conditions

The fourth approach—the *"soft" conditions* field of theory—according to Musterd and Murie, "asserts the importance of specific urban amenities that create an environment that attracts people who are key to the most promising economic activities for the economic development of the urban region."[18] Identifying exactly who these people are, is perhaps most closely identified with the work of Richard Florida and his notion of the "creative class." Florida notes that the distinguishing characteristic of the creative class is that its members engage in work whose function is to *create meaningful new forms*, and defines this class as consisting of two components:

1. The super-creative core—that is, scientists, engineers, university professors, artists, entertainers, actors designers, architects, and so forth, who engage in the highest order of creative work, in terms of producing new forms or designs that are readily transferable and widely useful
2. Creative professionals—working in a wide range of knowledge-intensive industries (e.g., high-tech sectors, financial services, legal and healthcare professionals, business management etc.), who engage in creative problem solving, drawing on complex bodies of knowledge to solve specific problems, typically requiring a high level of formal education and consequently a high level of human capital[19]

Linking to the cluster perspective briefly outlined above, Florida argues that this approach (in terms of capturing efficiencies generated from tight linkages between firms etc.) can also be explained in terms of locating to a specific place in order *to* "draw from concentrations of talented people who power innovation and economic growth. The ability to rapidly mobilize talent from such a concentration of people is a tremendous source of competitive advantage for companies in our time-driven and horizontal economy."[20] Florida emphasizes the *power of place* remains, but suggests that in this context, the "creative class" group is drawn to creative centers, not for the traditional economic reasons outlined in terms of "hard" conditions, but because they seek abundant high-quality amenities and experiences, an openness to diversity of all kinds, and above all else the opportunity to validate their identities as creative people.[21]

These "soft" amenity factors attracting the "creative class" to specific urban areas are in many ways vaguer and more subjective than the "hard" conditions mentioned above. However, Musterd and Murie note that this approach has been the subject of extensive critique, arising from the amorphous nature of "soft" factors, and the consequently weak empirical basis to the arguments underpinning this approach. However, they do acknowledge that throughout history the world's greatest cities have always been crucibles of innovation and creativity, including more recently those cities in the developing world, which manifest many of the issues outlined above relating to consumption adequacy for many of their populations. This is partly as Glaeser would suggest, precisely because slum dwellers are striving to improve their lot in life.[22] Perhaps the key issue relates to the extent to which such conditions fostering innovation and creativity can be actively constructed, or whether they emerge incrementally over time.

Linking this discussion back to the issue of resources mentioned in Chapter 2 in relation to the SDL of marketing, it could be argued that the "hard" conditions which may determine urban competitiveness are analogous to *operand* resources, whereas the notion of "soft" conditions has resonance with *operant* resources in that they are more dynamic and interactive and will affect how other (operand) resources are employed in order to achieve spatial competitive advantage. Certainly, there appears to be a developing consensus that investment in soft conditions is the most effective means to achieve competitive advantage—a view that has been termed the *New Conventional Wisdom*.[23]

According to the United Nations, the 21st century is the Century of the City[24] and notwithstanding many of the issues outlined above in relation to how cities are perceived, Gordon and Buck identify a shift "from seeing them as essentially problematic residues of nineteenth-and early twentieth-century ways of organizing industrial economies towards the idea that they could again be exciting and creative places in which to live and work."[25] They identify various imperatives in order to achieve this: (economic) competitiveness; (social) cohesion; (responsive) governance, and also (environmental) sustainability. It is outwith the scope of this short book to discuss these in detail, but Gordon emphasizes that if cities are to achieve their potential *positive, creative* role, then the interactions between economic, social, political, cultural, and environmental processes require an integrated, joined-up approach.

Intelligent Cities

Resonating with this notion of an integrated, joined-up approach, which emphasizes the importance integrating urban resources, is the concept of "intelligent cities." This a term used to describe those places combining factors such as organizational capacity, institutional leadership, and creativity to produce innovation in order to enhance competitiveness. Santinha and Castro define an intelligent city as:

> [A] city of knowledge where technological innovation and people's creativity are supported and encouraged, with strong institutional leadership and organizational capacity, creating the best possible conditions to increase competitiveness and sustainability.[26]

Crucial to this (and in doing so, hopefully overcoming some of the challenges raised by global competitiveness) are two key aspects. The first of these, linking to the issue of urban distinctiveness, is for cities to "develop a specialization pattern which can differentiate them from others." This can be accomplished by assembling a set of internal characteristics in terms of:

1. providing high-quality services and planning the territory in a way that its environment and urban design are attractive;
2. promoting a social and cultural milieu able to encourage creativity and efficiency amongst its citizens;
3. developing, maintaining, and attracting qualified and talented human resources with diverse skills and cultural backgrounds;
4. providing high-quality economic services;
5. facilitating the development of an organizational and technologically innovative environment capable of leveraging quality investment, thus promoting creativity and competitiveness among firms.

In addition, a city must also establish external connections, in terms of being able to:

1. be part of thematic networks which may enhance competitiveness and sustainability (analogous to the concept of clusters);

2. collect the necessary information to sustain the production of knowledge useful for its development;

3. disseminate information in a strategic way so that it can stand out as a destination.[27]

The second key aspect is the creation of governance mechanisms that allow city leaders to think strategically about development and intervene efficiently to meet challenges, both economic and social. Again, it is outwith the scope of this book to discuss the extensive debates of recent years on urban governance, but issues identified as specifically relating to this aspect include the debate as to whether delivery of public services should be the role of the public sector or private sector actors (via outsourcing etc.), the need for local/national governments to interact with society at different levels (including informal and formal actors/groups/organizations etc.) in order to tackle problems, and also whether the culture of local government should change from principally a service delivery body to that of an enabling one.[28] How individual cities deal with this array of issues will inevitably influence their ability to compete into the future.

Summary

The concept of consumption adequacy is inevitably connected to the notion of "unsettled times," as such periods of potential crisis and uncertainty have an impact on the ability of individuals to maintain their usual consumption behavior.

For many in the developed world, a reduced level of consumption adequacy during unsettled times may only be a temporary situation. However, for the majority of the world's population who make up the BoP, such a state of affairs is an ongoing aspect of their daily existence, and will inevitably impact on their ability to pursue a dignified and flourishing life.

Now that the majority of the world's population live in towns and cities, the marshaling of *urban* resources to help ensure the provision—through appropriate urban resource allocation and integration—of adequate conditions within cities and towns (and in particular those "megacities" of the developing world) to facilitate the provision of an appropriate level of consumption adequacy is becoming a key element of urban spatial competitiveness in an increasingly globalized economy.

In light of this, the next chapter moves on to consider in more detail the notion of cities and towns as service systems, through which as good a quality of life as possible can be provided to their inhabitants, and which are as resilient as possible in the face of "unsettled times."

Review and Discussion Questions

1. Why is the consumption behavior of the people at the bottom of the pyramid of potential importance to contemporary business organizations?
2. Why is the urban context important when considering the concept of consumption adequacy?
3. What factors could be classified as urban resources that could be used to develop a spatial competitive advantage?
4. What distinguishes between "hard" and "soft" conditions in the context of urban competition?
5. What kind of infrastructure could contribute to the creation of "intelligent cities"?

CHAPTER 4

A Service Science Perspective

Urban Service Systems

Introduction

If, as highlighted in the previous chapter, the need for an integrated, joined-up approach to urban resources—and related competitiveness—is accepted, then a service science approach, as described in Chapter 2, is one way to think about this.

This chapter takes a service science perspective relating to the urban context outlined in the previous chapter to consider how some of the issues relating to consumption adequacy and quality of life for inhabitants may be conceptualized. We consider the notion of cities as service systems in more detail relating to the resources encompassed within service systems—namely people, organizations, shared information, and technology. We end with a brief discussion of urban service system resiliency, which will be a key factor in the ability of urban systems to cope with "unsettled times," which will be the focus of subsequent chapters.

A Service(s) Perspective

Spatial entities (such as cities, and at a broader spatial scale, nations) have been identified as service systems.[1] Service systems are defined as "dynamic configurations of people, technologies, organizations and shared information that create and deliver value to customers, providers and other stakeholders."[2] This resonates with Turok's definition of cities as "complex adaptive systems comprising multitudes of actors, firms and other organisations forming diverse relationships and evolving together in order to develop place-based competitive advantage."[3]

This recent focus on service science is the latest manifestation of attempts to use the concepts and principles of service(s) management/marketing to more fully understand the nature of place marketing and management. For example, the servicescape concept[4] has obvious application in a wider urban place context. Warnaby has argued that service(s) marketing/management principles—and in particular the premises underpinning the service-dominant logic (SDL) of marketing—are a means by which the context specificity of places (which has led to the view that places need to be viewed as a special type of marketing) can be more fully incorporated into mainstream marketing theory.[5] Thus, to take one example, the Nordic School service logic, which views firms as facilitating the processes that support customers' value creation,[6] has been considered in the specific context of urban places by Warnaby and Davies, who adapted the servuction system model to cities and towns, showing how the integration of both physical and social resources of urban places may be integrated to facilitate perceived value-in-use by urban users/stakeholders.[7] Arguably, such applications of the service-oriented perspective will assume an increasing importance in place management/marketing practice.

Considering the above issues from a more specific resource integration perspective, it has been noted previously that "hard" and "soft" conditions for urban competitiveness are analogous to operand and operant resources mentioned in Chapter 2. This resource-based perspective could also be applied to the concept of place more generally. Discussing the nature and meaning of place is perhaps more suited to the discipline of geography rather than business and management, but it is instructive to briefly consider places through the lens of resource integration as it is of relevance for their conceptualization as service systems.

A Place Marketing Perspective

Considering how places could be viewed as "products," Cresswell and Hoskins argue that the notion of place simultaneously evokes two elements:

1. *Materiality* (in that a place has tangible form, manifested, for example, by discrete administrative boundaries, topography, built environment, and so forth)

2. A *"less concrete" realm of meaning*, relating to how people feel about and perceive the place. This of course, can vary across different people, groups, and institutions—relating to such factors as strength of attachment to the place, the longevity of association with the place, and so on—and may as a consequence be strongly contested[8]

In the place marketing literature, various authors have conceptualized places as "products" consisting of an array of contributory elements.[9] Drawing on the basic marketing notion of differing product levels (core, actual, augmented products), many conceptualizations of the urban place "product" have utilized core and supplementary/peripheral, or primary/secondary elements. These place product elements can be conceived of as resources to be deployed to construct an attractive place "product" aimed at specific market segments (i.e., tourists, inward investors, and so forth). Here, both operand and operant resources are relevant. Relating to Cresswell and Hoskins' notion of materiality, physical aspects (e.g., location, infrastructure) can be likened to oper*and* resources. More service-oriented elements (e.g., skills/character of the population, the cosmopolitan/bohemian nature of the place), can be likened to oper*ant* resources. Both types of resource can be deployed in order to motivate exchange.

Cresswell and Hoskins' notion of realm of meaning has resonance with the recent development of place branding as a practice and as a subject of academic study. In the context of places, this notion of realm of meaning can be linked to the concept of co-creation (discussed in Chapter 2). Thus, Aitken and Campelo see place brands as social constructions which are co-created among a wide array of stakeholders, not merely from the supply side (i.e., local administrations, place marketing/management agencies, and so forth), but also more collectively among all place stakeholders, through an iterative collaborative process which is culturally informed and contextually bound: as they state "[a] place brand by nature belongs to the place and its people."[10] Indeed, there is increasing recognition of the role of place residents as targets—and also creators—of place marketing/branding activities. Braun et al. identify various roles that residents may play:

1. as an integrated part of the place brand, through their characteristics and behavior;

2. as ambassadors, granting credibility to communicated messages; and
3. as citizens and voters, who are instrumental in the political legitimization of place branding.[11]

Principles derived from services marketing and service science can, therefore, be of utility in setting a context for the conceptualization of cities as service systems. The next section will consider the specifics of this in more detail.

Cities as Service Systems

As noted above, applying service(s) marketing/service science principles to a place context, cities could be conceptualized as a configuration of resources (both operand and operant) that can be integrated by an array of place stakeholders in an attempt to create spatial competitive advantage. Taking a broader service science perspective, the resources encompassed within service systems have been categorized as *people, organizations, shared information,* and *technology*.[12] Each of these inter-related elements is considered in more detail below.

People

Within cities there exists a multiplicity of different actors (individuals, formal and informal groups, associations, organizations, public administrations, and so forth) that—individually and collectively—will integrate their resources to create a place service system. From a place marketing perspective, addressing the question of who (co-)creates the place "product," Ashworth suggests three possible "producers."[13] The first two are:

1. the assembler of the various elements in a place product "package" (typically organizations such as tourism operators); and
2. governments and their agencies.

These "supply-side" actors, who—in isolation or in combination—integrate place-based resources at their disposal, can be considered as "value networks," defined by Lusch et al. as a spontaneously sensing and responding spatial and temporal structure of largely loosely coupled value proposing social and economic actors interacting through institutions and technology, to (1) co-produce service offerings, (2) exchange service offerings, and (3) co-create value.[14]

They state that value networks may interconnect and that individual value networks may nest within larger, more encompassing ones. This notion of functional/spatial "nesting" has parallels in a place context, where a city may be part of a wider region, economic cluster, or both. Moreover, within an individual place there may exist a variety of different (albeit most likely interconnected) value networks, each with a different remit, such as for example, tourism promotion, or attracting inward investment.

According to Ashworth, the third "producer" of an urban place product is the consumers themselves, who create their own unique product from the variety of services/amenities, and so on, available therein, with the place producer having little direct control over this process. Indeed, Ashworth argues for the primacy of the consumer as the place product creator. Considering this using the foundational premises (FPs) of SDL of marketing discussed in Chapter 2, there are a number of core SDL FPs that are manifest in a place context.

The SDL argues that the customer is always a co-creator of value (FP6) and that value is always uniquely and phenomenologically determined by the beneficiary (FP10). Those organizations/groups/local authorities who, from a more traditional perspective, could be regarded as creators of the place product would, using SDL parlance, only perform what Vargo and Lusch term an intermediate role through offering place value propositions arising from a particular assemblage of place product elements (FP7), which would be created through the integration of resources (i.e., place product elements) available within the place (FP9). Thus, the various place product elements constitute the means to an end, rather than the end in itself, in that place stakeholders will reside in/visit/locate to a particular place in order to realize the variety of benefits/experiences available therein. Moreover, the relative importance of place product elements will be determined by the consumer, in line with the SDL's FP10, and linking explicitly to the notion of place as realm of meaning.[15]

Organizations

The complexity of the mechanisms for place marketing has been identified as a factor that distinguishes this particular context; more specifically, relating to partnerships between public and private sector agencies/organizations. As noted in the last chapter, governance mechanisms and processes will have a potential impact on urban competitiveness. Thus, the process of value co-creation and resource integration in this context will inevitably arise from interaction and relationships. Such relational exchanges will occur not only with place stakeholders, but also between all the members of what van den Berg and Braun term the "strategic network," responsible for the place management/marketing effort. One of the specific characteristics of place marketing is the plethora of stakeholders from private, public, and voluntary sectors (often with competing agendas) that are involved in this activity. The consequent need for a consensual and inclusive approach to place marketing strategy making is emphasized.[16] Van den Berg and Braun stress the importance of "organizing capacity" defined as:

> [T]he ability to enlist all actors involved and, with their help, to generate new ideas and to develop and implement a policy designed to respond to fundamental developments and create conditions for sustainable development.[17]

Chandler and Vargo identify the importance of resources as owned or accessible by multiple actors and their role in facilitating actor interaction (in order to capitalize more optimally upon these resources). In this specific context, where resource (especially operand resource, such as finance) may be limited, the application of operant resources such as actor interaction and network development becomes more important. They stress the importance of context, defined as "a set of unique actors with unique reciprocal links between them,"[18] highlighting that context heterogeneity affects the efficacy of resource mobilization. This has particular resonance in an urban place context, where the *strategic network* which enables the *organizing capacity* to implement activities aimed at enhancing competitiveness, will inevitably reflect specific situations within particular locations.

Chandler and Vargo regard context as a multilevel conceptualization, incorporating:

1. *micro* (i.e., framing direct exchange between individual actors as part of dyads);
2. *meso* (i.e., framing more indirect exchange as it occurs among dyads within triads); and
3. *macro* (i.e., framing exchange as it occurs among triads, which may create complex networks).

Van den Berg and Braun identify three levels of (urban) place marketing, comprising:

1. the individual urban goods and services;
2. clusters of related services; and,
3. the urban agglomeration as a whole, which may be open to various interpretations, as different combinations of individual goods/services and clusters may be promoted to distinct market segments, and is mainly concerned with identity and image building for the urban place as a holistic entity.

Applying such conceptualizations relating to context using van den Berg and Braun's three levels of urban place marketing, then interaction between individual actors (i.e., micro level) might create individual place product elements such as tourism attractions, which might then be part of clusters to create an overall tourism offer (i.e., meso level), which can, through interaction with non-tourism-oriented (but nonetheless related) marketing actors, in turn be an element of a wider holistic product—the town/city as a whole (i.e., macro level). Given the inherent complexity of organizational mechanisms, these levels may be even more inter-related with individual clusters of elements being marketed by complex networks of actors. Moreover, Chandler and Vargo add another—*meta-context*—level, which introduces notions of time and replication, leading to institutionalization, and the ongoing nature of some place management/marketing initiatives suggests that relatively permanent ecosystems can be created, which become established as a valid element of urban management/marketing more generally.

The nature of this actor interaction could take various forms. Warnaby et al. identify three different types of interaction which are evident in this context:

1. Formal Interaction—that is, where there is ex officio representation of individuals/associations/organizations, and so forth on those formal groups and scheduled (often regular, periodic) meetings where activities relating to the management/marketing of places to achieve competitive advantage are planned

2. Informal Interaction—that is, participation of interested parties in less formal local networks, which may take the form of regular contact relating to updating others about activities undertaken, and so on

3. Initiative-Specific (or ad hoc) Interaction—that is, groups of actors coming together in groupings for a finite period to collaborate on specific initiatives (e.g., advertising/marketing communications activities, which may be time limited, such as seasonal promotional campaigns), and who then dissolve until such time as the group may reconvene (not necessarily with exactly the same membership) for the next time a specific activity is planned. Indeed, there may be a number of initiative-specific activities occurring simultaneously (each with a different constellation of stakeholders) in the same place[19]

This leads neatly to the third type of resource, namely, shared information.

Shared Information

Maglio and Spohrer emphasize the exchange of competence between members of a service system, and suggest that this may occur along at least four dimensions: *information sharing, work sharing, risk sharing,* and *goods sharing.* The relative importance of each may vary, but Maglio and Spohrer suggest that "it seems all four dimensions are present to some extent in almost all service systems."[20] The nature of the organizational mechanisms for place marketing with their high level of interaction (as mentioned above) obviously facilitates such exchange and sharing. Acknowledging this, Corsico introduces the metaphor of city as market, reflecting the fact that it is:

> [T]he milieu in which a system of trade, a network of relation-ships is valid. Moreover, it is a place of bargaining and negoti-ation, where the values traded are not restricted to those with a price tag.[21]

The urban place and its institutions, therefore, become the forum in which urban stakeholders communicate and (hopefully) reach some consensus as to future development. However, there is inevitably potential for tension and conflict, both within the "strategic network" and beyond this group to include those marginalized from any decision-making processes. Managing such potential conflict is a key element of place management and marketing.

Another aspect to this information sharing is linked to the concept of local embeddedness, related to the notion of "soft" conditions outlined in the previous chapter. Turok, in his discussion of place competitiveness identifies these more intangible skills, knowledge, and occupations associ-ated with/available in a place as a source of distinctiveness. This intangible character is, he states, associated with tacit knowledge and "soft skills" (e.g., initiative, communication, problem solving, and so on), and is also apparent in the trust and informal networks that can develop between place stakeholders.

Technology

From a service systems perspective, technology is defined as:

> [A]n accessible physical resource that does not have the ability to establish formal contractual relationships. It includes any human-made physical artefact or portion of the environment accessible to service system stakeholders.[22]

IfM and IBM consider technology in this context in terms of two properties:

1. *Physical* (i.e., the technology hardware)
2. *Codified conceptual* (i.e., shared information, and so on)

Service systems can own these properties, and provide access rights to others in order to enable value exchanges.

Indeed, Santinha and Castro argue that, if knowledge is the engine and information is the fuel of economic development, then information communication technology (ICT) could be seen as driving the process of innovation in terms of reducing the distance and time constraints in inter-personal and inter-institutional contacts and by reducing the complexity of exchanging and acquiring information. They regard the development of ICT-based services as an *enabling* factor—in other words, as the means to an end, rather than the end in itself. Moreover, they suggest that the importance of ICT increases in proportion with both the network of contacts and the complexity of the information exchange between those networks, which may be both within and between places.[23] In the context of service systems, the broad use of technology can be considered in terms of two key aspects:

1. Facilitating the operation of core urban services
2. Facilitating governance mechanisms

Facilitating the Operation of Core Urban Services

Dirks et al. in an IBM publication on *Smarter Cities* argue that the key basis for urban competitive differentiation is (linking back to Florida's "creative class" thesis) the talent pool available within the place. The skills, aptitude, knowledge, creativity, and innovation of an urban workforce have become, they argue, increasingly important drivers of economic growth and activity, and the attraction of high-skilled individuals is a key task. They suggest that to accomplish this, cities should focus on four core areas: reducing congestion in the transport system; improving emergency response and reducing crime; improving education delivery and streamlining government services; and improving access to patient-centric healthcare. They go on to argue that if cities are to maximize their competitive position, then those responsible for their management need to cultivate a cross-systems perspective which incorporates all these core systems (and indeed, others) in order to optimize their position. One important means to achieve this is to develop and apply information technologies to improve these core city systems by focusing on "leveraging the power of the vast amounts of real-world data they already collect about the behavior patterns of the city's people and systems, taking care to equip their systems with three basic levels of ability:

1. Collect and manage the right kind of data.
2. Integrate and analyze the data.
3. Based on advanced analysis, optimize the system to achieve desired system behaviors."[24]

Facilitating Governance Mechanisms

Santinha and Castro suggest the existence of four possible different levels of ICT use by local/regional governments in their governance mechanisms, which could be regarded as facilitating their operation as "service systems":

1. Level 1—Providing web information of a passive and unidirectional nature (usually relating to services provided to the local populace, spatial planning issues, and so forth), with the primary purpose of facilitating the provision of information to relevant place stakeholders
2. Level 2—Using ICT for interaction and transaction purposes with citizens and other institutions (for example, in relation to submission of forms payments, or the issuing of licenses/permits etc.). At this stage using ICT can "be very helpful in improving coordination and diminishing the bureaucracy connected with administrative procedures and transactions, qualifying and improving efficiency and effectiveness between the government and citizens or other

institutions, and linking services of local/regional governments with other services"

3. Level 3—Using ICT in promoting interaction with citizens and other institutions so that full participation in policy design and decision making is granted. This will involve the development of adequate systems for information dissemination, public discussion, and information collection inherent in any consultative process. Such a process, according to Santinha and Castro "produces qualitative changes in governance mechanisms, namely with respect to a greater transparency and legitimacy of public policy design and decision making providing strong conditions for consensus building"

4. Level 4—Using ICT to bring many participants into the public policy domain. This is similar to level three, but would also involve developing complementary initiatives to provide stakeholders not only with the knowledge to inform their participation in policy design processes, but also the necessary mechanisms to organize collectively and thereby increase their capacity for participation and mobilization in their collective interests[25]

Urban Service Systems and Quality of Life

Thus cities and other urban places can be conceptualized as service systems—constituting a variety of components whereby urban resource is organized and integrated to deliver growth and place-based competitive advantage.

Core Service Systems

Service systems are complex adaptive systems, which according to IfM and IBM can also be thought of as a type of "system of systems" containing internal smaller service systems as well as being contained in a larger service system.[26] In an urban context, Dirks et al. identify a set of smaller internal urban service systems—termed *core* systems—which they argue play a crucial role in attracting and expanding skills and innovation—factors critical to urban competitiveness.[27] These core systems relate to transport, government services and education, public safety and health, and have a profound influence on urban attractiveness.

Kotler et al. highlight the important role that such infrastructure plays in place marketing activities:

> [I]nfrastructure investments, whether in getting more out of existing facilities or in making new investments that meet multiple needs and priorities, may be the most critical decision that places make in improving their competitive position.[28]

Short and Kim identify "solid infrastructure"—incorporating transportation, telecommunications, local gas and electricity, and so on—as one of the major themes of city representation in the United States of America.[29] Gold also emphasizes the importance of transport infrastructure in this context, and Ward makes the point that in place promotion messages, "[i]nfrastructure is invariably ideal."[30]

Quality of Life

Kotler et al. use the term "infrastructure marketing" to describe a focus on such issues, and consider the absence of appropriate place infrastructure as problematic, with implications for quality of life, long recognized as an important element of place marketing messages. Indeed, in this specific place context, the concept of *quality of life* has significant implications not only for the lived experience of urban populations, but also for promotion and marketing. Rogerson identifies various ways in which good ratings in the various place quality of life league tables that exist have been long used by towns and cities for promotional purposes. This can be in terms of, for example, raising a city's profile in national and international economic arenas and challenging a stereotypical image of the city as being an area of industrial decline, and moreover, also where poor ratings have been used to attract state expenditure and the redistribution of surpluses through state and national governments or via supranational (e.g., European Union) assistance programs.[31]

Quality of life is a multifaceted concept. In a review of previous research into attributes of quality of life, Rogerson lists a multitude of factors, but emphasizes that:

> [W]hilst the list of specific elements to be incorporated into a definition of quality of life varies, the focus is consistently on factors such as physical environment, climate, pollution, crime and social facilities linked to education, health.

He goes on to state that the view of quality of life employed by many has become narrowly defined, largely arising from the use of the concept to commodify the city in an attempt to lure capital via inward investment, and its associated job creation, and so on. This privileging of capital's notion of quality of life, he argues, has important consequences for "the shape of the urban quality of life on offer in the contemporary city."[32] For example, there are alternative ways for conceiving quality of life that consider life satisfaction and happiness which have been given too little emphasis, although it should be noted that there has been recent research on happiness which addresses some of these issues.[33]

Research into items which have been identified as being perceived as the most important in people's current lives has identified (in descending order) the following:

1. Relationship with family/relatives
2. Own health
3. Health of someone else
4. Finances/housing/standard of living
5. Relationships with other people
6. Availability of work/able to work
7. Other (including crime, politics, happiness/well-being)
8. Social life/leisure activities
9. Conditions at work/job satisfaction
10. Education
11. Religion/spiritual life
12. Environment (pollution, rubbish, noise, safety, cleanliness)[34]

Looking down this list, there is some resonance with Nussbaum's "central capabilities" (required in order to pursue a "dignified and minimally flourishing life") mentioned in the previous chapter.[35] Indeed, it could be argued that the typical use of urban quality of life rating scales is largely one-dimensional, and consequently issues of access and (ine)quality of provision of urban services/facilities are neglected. As Rogerson states:

> Whilst some insight into differential quality of life can be evaluated through measures of access and provision, it is only when dimensions of experience are added that the 'city ratings' will be more than advertising hype and meaningful to people.[36]

A key issue therefore, is the ability of urban service systems to deliver an equitable level of service and infrastructure provision for all residents on an ongoing basis, and also in times of stress and crisis—in other words, during what we have termed unsettled times. The ability (or otherwise) of systems to adequately cope in these circumstances will be a function of their inherent *resilience*.

Urban Service System Resilience

The UK Cabinet Office, part of whose remit is to ensure national infrastructure is maintained in order to ensure effective provision of nine essential sectors (i.e., food, energy, water, communications, transport health, emergency services, government, and finance), upon which daily life in the United Kingdom depends, defines resilience as "the ability of assets, networks and systems to anticipate, absorb, adapt to and/or rapidly recover from a disruptive event." However, there is an acknowledgment that resilience "is more than an ability to bounce back and recover from adversity and extends to the broader adaptive capacity gained from an understanding of the risks and uncertainties in our environment."[37] It argues that resilience is secured through various activities and components—the four principal strategic components it identifies as resistance, reliability, redundancy, and response and recovery, each of which is discussed in more detail below, and will be elaborated on in Chapter 6.[38]

Resistance

Resistance is focused on preventing damage or disruption to the system by providing the strength or protection to resist the hazard or its primary impact. The Cabinet Office identifies some potential weaknesses in resistance strategies in that they are often developed to protect against the kind of events that have been previously expected or those predicted to occur based on historic records. In a climatic context, for instance, the increasing frequency of occurrence of "once in a hundred years"-type extreme weather events highlights the potential for disruptive events to exceed the standards provided for protection, thereby causing the system to be strained or broken, and "unsettled times" to occur more frequently and with greater impact than would have been the case otherwise.

Reliability

Reliability is concerned "with ensuring that the infrastructure components are inherently designed to operate under a range of conditions and hence mitigate the damage or loss from an event." Again, the point is made that reliability strategies may focus only on events within a specified range, and as a consequence very extreme events may be inadequately prepared for, thereby leading to more significant wider and prolonged impacts. As the Cabinet Office states: "Reliability cannot therefore be guaranteed, but deterioration can sometimes be managed at a tolerable level until full services can be restored after the event"—thereby mitigating the full impact of unsettled times.

Redundancy

Redundancy is concerned with "the design and capacity of the network or system," and is concerned with such factors as the availability of backup installations or spare capacity, which would enable normal operations to be diverted to alternative parts of the system/network, thereby ensuring continuity. This might lead to an initial loss of performance until the contingency measures can be brought into operation. An important issue here is the existence of spare capacity in the system. As the Cabinet Office states: "The resilience of networks reduces when running at or near capacity, although in some sectors or organisations it is recognised that it may not always be feasible to operate with significant spare capacity within the network."

Response and Recovery

This, as the name implies, aims to facilitate and enable a fast and effective *response to* and *recovery from* disruptive events. The Cabinet Office suggests that the effectiveness of this element is determined by the thoroughness of planning efforts in advance of events. A distinction is made between response and recovery, in that response relates to the ability to quickly restore service provision (arising partly from a good understanding of the potential weaknesses within networks/systems), and recovery is considered in pre-event planning in order to explore opportunities to reduce future risks, build resilience, or both during the recovery stage.

In summary, the Cabinet Office states that infrastructure resilience is provided through two inter-related aspects:

1. Good design of the system to ensure that it has the required resistance, reliability, and redundancy (i.e., spare capacity) in order to cope.
2. By establishing good organizational resilience to provide the ability, capacity, and capability to respond and recover from disruption. This is achieved through business operations and appropriate support for continuity management.

Summary

This chapter has considered the concept of cities as service systems, highlighting that concepts from the service(s) marketing literature have much utility in conceptualizing urban places in this way. The elements of service systems—people, organizations, shared information, and technology—are all applicable in the context of places. Indeed, the multiplicity of potential actors and organizations responsible for the operation of urban service systems arising from the inherent complexity of places (and especially urban places), requires a coordinated and systematic approach to their management, if a good quality of life is to be delivered for residents, and also, if as resilient a system as possible is to be created. This notion of urban system resilience is of particular saliency in periods of what we have termed "unsettled times," and it is to the operation of urban service systems in such times that the remainder of the book now turns.

Review and Discussion Questions

1. In what ways can a service(s) perspective inform thinking about cities as service systems?
2. Can places be considered as "products" to be marketed?
3. What are the key elements of an urban service system?
4. How might effective urban service systems contribute to the quality of life of city dwellers?
5. What are the key constituents of service system resiliency?

CHAPTER 5

Urban Service Systems in Unsettled Times

Introduction

In the previous chapter, we discussed the notion of cities as service systems. Within this context, we recognized the multiplicity of actors involved in these systems: people, organizations, shared information, and technology, and acknowledged the need for a coordinated and systematic approach to the management of issues which give rise to unsettled times in these environments.

In this chapter, we introduce three case studies, each of which illustrate different types of unsettled times. It is the intention of this chapter to simply describe these case studies which are subsequently analyzed in Chapter 6. As we pointed out in the Introduction, our focus in this book is upon unsettled times which arise from environmental and climatic conditions. But just how important are unsettled times associated with these conditions? The Centre for Research on the Epidemiology of Disasters (CRED) provides us with some sense of how important these conditions are in a global context.[1]

CRED maintains a publicly accessible database of what it terms "disasters," broadly consistent with our theme of unsettled times.[2] CRED categorizes disasters into three areas:

1. Natural disasters, for example, earthquakes
2. Technological disasters, for example, a nuclear incident
3. Complex emergencies, for example, a hazardous material or transportation incident (chemical spill)

This database is populated by data collected from United Nations (UN) agencies, national governments, insurance organizations, and the media.

For a disaster to be entered onto the database there are four criteria which need to be fulfilled:

1. Deaths of 10 or more people are reported.
2. The number of people affected reaches 100, or above.
3. A state of emergency is declared.
4. International assistance is called for.

Of the three categories, natural disasters account for the most significant number of "unsettled" times. These natural disasters might include:

1. biological, for example, the spread of germs and toxic substances;
2. climatological, for example, blizzards and snow storms;
3. geophysical, for example, earthquakes;
4. hydrological, for example, tsunami;
5. meteorological incidents, for example, hurricanes.

That said, whilst natural disasters may numerically account for the greater number of incidents, these disasters do not occur in a vacuum. Often they provide the trigger to a man-made disaster: an earthquake (natural disaster) prompting the collapse of buildings and infrastructure (man-made disaster), leading to multiple deaths.

To begin our review of unsettled times, we focus upon the floods that took place in Queensland Australia during the latter part of 2010 and early part of 2011. These floods affected multiple service systems, on separate occasions, in a number of ways. We follow this up with two studies of complex emergencies arising from climatic and environmental conditions. First, the earthquake and tsunami which hit Japan in 2011 is detailed. Second, the earthquakes which hit Christchurch, New Zealand in September 2010 and February 2011 are introduced. Each case study follows a similar format. It begins with an outline of the contextual setting and an overview of the threat under investigation. The subsequent review is structured to take account of the impact of the threat upon what Dirks et al. define as "core systems":

1. Transport services
2. Local government/public services

3. Education services
4. Health services
5. Utility services[3]

The chapter concludes taking account of how the multiple actors involved (citizen; public sector; business sector; and third sector) responded to the threats that arose.

Case Study 1: Floods, Queensland Australia (late 2010 and early 2011)

Context: Australia, officially the commonwealth of Australia, is the world's sixth largest country by area and includes mainland Australia, Tasmania, and a number of smaller islands. It is a continent of approximately 7.68 million square km (2.97 million square miles), broadly equivalent in land mass to the United States of America, minus Hawaii and Alaska. There are several climatic zones and three time zones. Summer falls from December to February. Urban service systems utilize natural landscapes which include desert habitats, rainforests, and beaches. Each system gives rise to distinct flora and fauna including the kangaroo, the koala, the wombat, and the platypus. The most recent population census of 2011 indicates population numbers to be in the region of 22,620,600[4] which places Australia as the most populous country in Oceania. It is however, one of the least densely populated countries in the world, 2.9 people per square km. The coastal areas are the most densely populated with Sydney and Melbourne home to around 8,000 people per square km. Five Australian cities have a population of more than a million people:

1. Sydney (4.4 million)
2. Melbourne (4 million)
3. Brisbane (2.1 million)
4. Perth (1.7 million)
5. Adelaide (1.2 million)

Canberra, the capital of Australia is home to 358,600 people. There are five states (New South Wales; Victoria; Queensland; Western Australia; South Australia), each with their own government administration.

Australia is a continent of contrasts, with Western Australia experiencing droughts, wildfires (linked to both drought conditions and arson), cyclones, and floods in recent years. This case study focuses upon events which happened in the state of Queensland, Eastern Australia. With a population exceeding 4 million, Queensland is Australia's second largest state. Queensland is home to the Great Barrier Reef and in excess of 200 National Parks covering 6.5 million hectares. Brisbane, the capital of Queensland has a population of over 2 million people. More than half of the state's population lives within the greater metropolitan area of Brisbane. The urban service system in this area is particularly complex. It includes three power stations, responsible for generating around half of Queensland's electricity capacity, an extensive water infrastructure, and a transport infrastructure which includes road (national and state highways), rail, seaport, and airport. Industry is dominated by manufacturing, engineering, and industrial services. The formal education sector is characterized by small schools and customized education for those geographically unable to reach mainstream education because of isolation.

Threat to the Urban Service System

In late December 2010 and early January 2011, an unusually strong "La Nina," a periodic climatic phenomenon that increases rainfall in the Western Pacific, hit the Australian coastline and Queensland interior leading to a "superstorm." By the 3rd of January 2011, 22 multiple urban service systems had been devastated by floods. In Rockhampton, floodwaters reached 30 feet, affecting an estimated 1,400 homes. Toowoomba, west of Queensland's state capital Brisbane, was subsequently hit with a flash flood which was regularly described in the media as an inland tsunami, the wave reaching 26 feet in places. This flood, accompanied by a wave of mud, water, and debris, left 12 people dead and 72 people missing. Local wildlife was extensively displaced and forced to collect together on higher ground. By Monday 10th January, almost 600 mm (2 feet) of rainfall had fallen in some places and approximately 1 million square km (385,000 square miles) of Queensland was declared to be a flood disaster zone. By the 12th of January, residents of Australia's third largest city, Brisbane, were warned to prepare for the worst floods in more than a century. The entire population of the suburb Forest Hill (approximately 300 people) were airlifted to safety. However, the devastation was not yet over. By the beginning of February 2011, fears of a cyclone, subsequently named Cyclone Yasi, prompted multiple responses. These included a stretch of coastline, some 190 miles long, being put on alert, the closure of Townsville and Cairns airports, the cutting of power to over 90,000 homes, and the recall of troops in preparation for mass mobilization to aid international disaster relief.

Types of Disruption

In this case study it is the core systems (identified by Dirks et al.) of transport services, local government/public services, health services and utility services, which received the most widespread media coverage. Education, whilst undoubtedly affected by unsettled times, was seldom referred to within the study datasets. We return to possible reasons for this absence in Chapter 6.

Transport Services

State transport services were widely affected by flood deluges. Road links, at both local and national levels, rail lines and airport runways, all submerged by floodwaters, ceased to function. The intensity of floodwaters caused the collapse of buildings, with mud, cars, and other debris being carried along both local and national routeways. Airports, the regional hub for commercial traffic, were closed for business, compromising both the receipt of produce for internal consumption and the dispatch of goods to the international community. Australia is the fourth largest exporter of wheat. At the time of the flooding, an estimated 8–10 million tonnes of wheat and barley crops were waiting to be harvested in Queensland and New South Wales. As a result of these unsettled times, wheat prices increased which in turn led to a hike in bread prices. Agriculture was heavily affected, with large areas of farming land on flood plains. The cost of fresh produce including bananas, mangoes, tomatoes, pumpkin, and sweet potato subsequently increased by as much as fourfold. The devastation caused by Cyclone Yasi led to the shutdown of Townsville and

Cairns airports. The city of Bundaberg closed its port leading to disrupted shipments of sugar which was particularly problematic given the world position of Australia as a leading world exporter of sugar.

Local Government/Public Services

From the beginning of the crisis, in December 2010, the public sector was to play a central role in the management of the disaster. A state of natural disaster was declared in 41 of Queensland's 73 municipalities. Reports published on December 30th 2010 noted that at least 1,000 people had been evacuated from their homes in Queensland with two Blackhawk helicopters scrambled to help to relocate all 300 people living in the town of Theodore. Forced evacuations were put into place across all the towns and cities most affected, both for safety reasons, and also to clear the area to allow personnel, police, and essential services, to search for missing persons. Residents were provided with instructions on what to take with them to evacuation centers: torches, matches, radios, medication, birth, and marriage certificates. They were directed to emergency shelters with the expectation of a 1-week long stay. Media reports place 4,000 people as crowded into evacuation centers, with whole families and towns evacuated. As the crisis continued, thousands of office and hotel workers were told not to risk their lives by going to work and more police services personnel were moved into locations to deal with fears of looting.

Health Services

Health services can be considered a central component within an urban service system. The disruption to these services throughout the towns and cities in Queensland was considerable, with health centers flooded, medications inaccessible, and health service professionals shifted to focus upon emergency cases rather than elective procedures. Additionally the floods brought their own distinct health problems above and beyond those ordinarily experienced within the service system. The floodwaters led to plagues of dangerous pests, trapping spiders and resulted in an invasion of locusts, snakes, mice, frogs, crocodiles, and sharks in Queensland. Residents were warned to be vigilant in looking out for crocodiles, alligators, snakes, possums, and koalas which might be displaced from their usual habitats and seeking refuge. Floodwaters also gave rise to infestations of mosquitoes and sand flies causing problems above and beyond the norm. Serious health concerns were raised as rivers of stinking brown muddy water and overflowing septic tanks posed serious dangers to public health. Holidaymakers were warned to avoid camp sites.

Utility Services

Power supplies took two particular hits during these unsettled times. First, in anticipation of a pending flood, companies cut power supplies to likely affected areas on safety grounds. This was widely reported to be the case in Queensland, where large areas of Brisbane city center had their power supplies cut off for protective reasons. Second, however, the surge of floodwaters in Rockhampton, Brisbane, and Toowoomba took the authorities off-guard and led to the severe unplanned disruption of power supplies with 4,000 homes losing power entirely. These homes inevitably included the elderly and vulnerable members of the community, less able to cope with the loss of essential facilities.

Types of Response

In the immediate aftermath of the first wave of flooding, citizens, local government/public services, businesses, and the third sector (also known as the not-for-profit, or charitable sector) utilized resources, often quite unusual ones, to assist with the recovery process.

Citizen Responses

Multiple examples of individual and collective actions, which contributed in different ways to the recovery processes, were reported in the media. These include:

1. the actions of community members who helped teachers in a local primary school to move computers and smart boards higher up in the school building, away from the worst flood damaged areas;

2. the endeavors of a tugboat captain who managed to race up the Brisbane River and prevent a massive chunk of concrete from smashing into one of the city's main bridges;

3. the community spirit of Clive Palmer, described as a coal magnate and one of Australia's richest men, whose helicopter was scrambled to rescue 60 people from floodwaters in northwest Brisbane;

4. the actions of midwife Carol Weeks from the United Kingdom who, on holiday in Cairns during Cyclone Yasi, successfully delivered a baby at a storm shelter;

5. the actions of local people who helped to set up relief centers, donate caravans, shift tonnes of mud and wash down the silt from the floors and walls of other resident's homes.

Local Government/Public Services Responses

Public sector responses to the disaster can be reviewed from two angles:

1. The national response
2. The local response

At the national level, the response to the 2011 floods was coordinated by Queensland Government, Department of Local Government, Community Recovery and Resilience. Prime Minister Julia Gillard announced a payment of up to A$1,000 per person to Queenslanders who had lost their homes through the flooding. Other heads of state, the UK Prime Minister David Cameron for instance, directed their offers of support through this route speaking directly with the Australian Prime Minister to offer any help needed. At the local level, Anna Bligh, Queensland's premier, days into the flooding, announced multiple responses to the disaster including:

1. the establishment of a task force to be led by an army general. The aim of this task force was to develop a flood recovery plan which would prioritize road and rail repairs to help to rejuvenate regional economies;

2. the operation of evacuation centers. A number of these centers were set up including one at the University of Rockhampton which was able to accommodate 1,500 people for 10 days;

3. the preparatory actions of four army Blackhawk helicopters and a Chinook ready to make food drops to isolated properties, communities, and farms;

4. the mobilization of community volunteers asked by police to fill sandbags;

5. the assistance of locals owning small boats and helicopters capable of ferrying people and emergency supplies around;

6. the call-up of military helicopters to deliver medical supplies, including snake-bite antidotes and to assist in the search and rescue of survivors;

7. the introduction of a flood tax to help to rebuild homes and public infrastructure.

The pivotal role played by the public sector is perhaps best illustrated by the words of evacuee Reg Wilson who, like many, was reticent to leave his home, "A man [policeman] came along in a car with a gun on his hip and said 'You need to be out of here by 5 o'clock.' When a man with a gun talks to you like that, you get out."[5] The authority of a law enforcing agency meant that it was possible to clear areas to allow search and rescue operations to continue unhindered.

Business Responses

One mechanism for returning a degree of stability to a destination in the aftermath of unsettled times, is to convey the message that not all have been affected. Tourism operators in Brisbane sought to do this by inviting visitors to Brisbane, the Gold Coast, Sunshine Coast, and Fraser Coast to post pictures on Facebook pages demonstrating the region to be functioning normally. Tourism activity is an important part of the Australian economy in general, and the Queensland economy in particular. In 2012, Queensland received approximately 18 million domestic overnight visitors, generating around $13.5 billion in spending. In addition, approximately 2 million international visitors are recorded as spending $3.8 billion.[6]

Third Sector Responses

The third sector played a prominent role in raising money to support flood victims and the region more generally. Celebrities, particularly drawn from the sporting (cricket and tennis) and music industries, dominated media coverage regularly utilizing social media, often Twitter, to share their fundraising activities. These activities included:

1. an auctioning of winning Ashes[7] shirts and cricket bats by the England cricket team to raise money for the appeal fund;
2. an auctioning of Ashes memorabilia by cricketer Kevin Pietersen to raise money for flood victims;
3. a donation of part of the match fees by the England and Australian cricket teams to raise money for flood victims;
4. the staging of exhibition matches by international tennis stars Roger Federer and Rafael Nadal to raise money for flood victims;
5. donations made by fellow celebrities including pop singer Kylie Minogue and calls for others, similarly placed, to do so too.

But it was not only celebrities who played a vital role in the immediate aftermath of the flooding; a number of charities (the Red Cross, the Salvation Army, and St John Ambulance) played a central role in supporting the set-up and operation of the evacuation centers where many residents, holidaymakers, and homeless people were forced to take refuge.

Case Study 2: Earthquake/Tsunami, Japan 2011

Context: Located in Eastern Asia, between the North Pacific Ocean and the Sea of Japan, east of the Korean peninsula, the Japanese archipelago consists of four main islands—Honshu, Hokkaido to the north, Shikoku across the Inland sea, and Kyushu to the southwest. The islands cover a total area of 377,915 square km, making them collectively the 42nd largest country in the world. Their coastline covers nearly 30,000 km and their climate varies: tropical in the south, and cool and temperate in the north. Around 75% of the country is extremely mountainous. The knock-on consequences of this are that Japan's people, factories, farming, housing, and public facilities are crammed into two-fifths of the landmass, with 67% of the population living in urban environments. This places Japan as the most densely populated nation in the world. With a negligible mineral resource base, the import of coal, oil, and gas is high. Reliance upon the service sector for gross domestic product (GDP) is also high. Japan is governed by a parliamentary government with a constitutional monarchy. There are 47 administrative divisions (prefectures), each with a governor.

Threat to the Urban Service System

On 11th March 2011, an earthquake registering a magnitude of 9.0, struck 43 miles off the northeast coast of Honshu, Japan's most populous island. This triggered a 15–20 m high tsunami (a Japanese word meaning "harbor wave"), lasting in excess of 4 minutes. This was the fifth most powerful ever recorded. It travelled 6 miles inland and shifted Japan 8 feet closer to America. Questions surrounding "have we done something wrong to nature?" were raised in the wake of the humanitarian crisis which followed. The threat to the service systems extended beyond the natural disaster and spread to the urban environment, more specifically engulfing the nuclear industry base at the heart of the Japanese energy provision. The stability of one nuclear site in particular, Fukushima, generated considerable concern with international media reports dominated by fears of radiation leakages and possible reactor plant meltdowns.

Types of Disruption

In this case study, once again it is the core systems (described by Dirks et al.) of transport services, local government/public services, health services, and utility services, which received the most widespread media coverage. Education was seldom referred to within the study datasets, other than to recognize the regular drills that schools pursue anyway in anticipation of such unsettled times. Little attempt was made to comment upon the success, or otherwise, of these drills.

Transport Services

The disaster led to immediate and severe damage to transportation and communications infrastructure. Fires engulfed cars, buses, trains, and ships. Airport operations were compromised, particularly as aftershocks continued to threaten the stability of runways. A cruise ship sank, four trains disappeared, and fishing trawlers were dragged into whirlpools created in the immediate aftermath of the tsunami. What makes this case study particularly apposite is that it aptly illustrates both the indirect, and longer-term, consequences a disaster may pose. In the immediate aftermath of the disaster, car manufacturers Toyota, Honda, and Nissan, along with electronics manufacturer Sony, suspended production at their Japanese sites. Shutdowns were linked to a lack of supplies, the need to repair facilities, a lack of power, and the need to ensure the safety of the workforce. Economists voiced concerns that closures, however temporary, would lead to a shrinking of economic output, yet underestimated the full economic consequences which were to be felt for some time, and beyond Japan. In the United Kingdom for instance, months after the tsunami, Honda was forced to cut production at its Swindon factory due to a shortage of parts, ordinarily dispatched from Japan. Changes in car production also had knock-on consequences for car-hire companies who were forced to raise rental prices for holidaymakers due to reduced fleet sizes.

Local Government/Public Services

More than half a million Japanese residents were displaced by the disaster, many communities forced to live in school gymnasiums with questions asked about why earthquake evacuation points were located so close to the shoreline. The unanticipated nuclear threat which emerged through the disaster prompted the need for particular direct government action which is unique to this case study: residents within a 100 miles radius of the threatened Fukushima nuclear plant were evacuated as a precaution and 160 military personnel were dispatched by the Japanese Government to the plant to assess the situation and to determine an appropriate response.

Health Services

Health provision was severely disrupted by the disaster. In addition to the reported initial loss of 9,000 people, three workers suffered radiation exposure at the Fukushima nuclear power plant with multiple residential communities in the locality seeking medical support over similar fears. The Japanese onsen, otherwise known as hot spring spas, were also threatened as the earthquake affected the water table. As well as attracting millions of visitors each year to the region, these spas play an important role in the health and well-being of the local population.

Utility Services

Water, food, and fuel were all severely compromised by the disaster. Some 1.4 million homes suffered an immediate loss of access to water, whilst more than 4 million homes lost electricity. By June, 3 months after the initial disaster, 124,000 residents were still living in evacuation centers, drawing upon collective, rather than individual utility services. Sanitation was to prove a particularly difficult area to manage. Fearful of the effects of the disaster upon the sewerage systems and the water table, residents were advised not to use the normal sanitary facilities, but instead to utilize plastic bags for toiletry needs. This advice generated considerable comment within media reports as residents expressed concern over the hygiene implications that might subsequently arise. Problems were also encountered in the telecommunications sector. The hit to the country's power supply resulted in a failure of phone voice services in the northeast and an inability of Sony Ericsson's smart phones to function at all. That said, data services linked to e-mail functions did allow some residents to maintain contact with family and friends during the crisis.

Types of Response

Citizen Responses

Collective, collegial responses from citizens were to dominate the media coverage of both the immediate, and longer-term, disaster aftermath:

1. In Senen General Hospital, two doctors, without water and electricity, and only limited supplies of food and drugs, kept services operating for 113 patients.

2. Shiogama, 7 miles northeast of Sendai, essentially functioned as a small independent republic post-disaster. Administered by a librarian Noriko Sato, thousands of people gathered in the local primary school, to share their own supplies with each other, at a time when the town felt "forgotten," the local police station deserted.

3. Minami Sanriku, a fishing community, sheltered 700 people in their local gym. Media reports highlighted how, even during breakdowns in service systems, the local population maintained standards: dinner queues were well organized and residents both polite and respectful, removing shoes as at home. Local doctors and nurses kept services operational whilst the two roads into the town were cleared.

Local Government/Public Services Responses

Within 4 minutes of the earthquake, international media sources reported that Prime Minister Naoto Kan had established a special disaster response unit within his office and taken over leadership of the relief activity. The relief effort was extensive:

1. Within the first hour, civil defense forces, police officers, and other rescue workers were on their way to the afflicted areas.

2. Within the first two days, 50,000 military personnel were mobilized and 26 million single-meal portions of essential foodstuff, nearly 8 million bottles of drinking water, and 230,000 boxes of basic medicines were dispatched.

3. Local authorities requested prefabricated homes to act as temporary accommodation.

4. In Tokyo, the deputy mayor dispatched 384,000 blankets and 9,000 portable toilets to affected areas.

5. A major highway running through the Tohoku region, at the heart of the disaster, was reopened after only 2 weeks.

6. The airport at Sendai was reopened in a third of the expected time after American Troops repaired the runway.
7. The bullet train, the Shinkansen, linking Tokyo and the Tohoku region reopened within 6 weeks.
8. Within a month of the tsunami and earthquake, widespread formal reconstruction work began.
9. By May 2011, over 160,000 personnel had been deployed and more than 26,000 people rescued.

The effort extended beyond the Japanese government and included the deployment of search and rescue teams from Australia, New Zealand, South Korea, and the United States of America. Singapore and Britain deployed urban search and rescue teams. Switzerland sent 25 rescue and medical experts. Both immediate and longer-term policies were put into place. These included efforts to restore longer-term confidence in Japanese food with the Agriculture, Forestry and Fisheries ministry submitting an application to United Nations Educational, Scientific and Cultural Organization (UNESCO) to consider Japan's food culture as an intangible cultural asset. Also, to encourage international tourists to return to the three regions hit hardest, a waiving of visa fees for a period of 5 years was introduced to encourage visitation.

Business Responses

In addition to central government actions, private businesses set about assisting with the relief effort. In Tokyo for instance, the instant noodle manufacturer Nissin forwarded one million packets of noodles and "kitchen cars" equipped with stoves and water to affected areas. Within a month of the disaster many factories started to reopen, with production lines beginning to run. Local businesses fought on to preserve and capitalize upon their remaining damaged stock: the owner of one family shoe business for instance, set about hand washing all the damaged shoe stock, selling them on for 500 yen, instead of the original 10,000 yen. Businesses collectively responded to calls to unplug their lighting displays, helping to conserve energy and support rolling blackout schemes.

Third Sector Responses

Once again, efforts to raise money to support victims, and the region more generally, generated a considerable amount of media coverage:

1. The Nippon Music Foundation for instance, auctioned one of the best preserved Stradivarius violins in aid of the disaster relief program, raising $9.8 million, a third more than previously paid for the instrument.
2. Alongside distributing hygiene equipment, first-aid kits, masks, school uniforms, toys and games, and back-to-school kits, the Save the Children Fund established spaces across Japan where children could express themselves and play.
3. British-based charity Shelterbox, through their response to humanitarian disasters program, distributed tents and other vital supplies, particularly geared toward minimizing the spread of waterborne diseases which the Japanese population were considered to be particularly vulnerable to.
4. The Japan Philharmonic Orchestra played to a UK audience with all proceeds going toward the disaster appeal.

Celebrities, again drawn particularly from the sporting and music industries, dominated the literature, communicating their condolences via Twitter, and pledging financial support for those affected:

1. Japanese golfer Ryo Ishikawa pledged his season's winnings to the earthquake relief fund, with Korean KJ Choi and Bubba Watson offering similar donations.
2. Lady Gaga designed a wristband with all proceeds to the disaster relief fund.
3. Giorgio Armani incorporated Japanese silks and cherry blossom themes into his Paris collection, subsequently donating the entire collection of clothes to the disaster appeal.

Case Study 3: Earthquake, Christchurch New Zealand (September 2010 and February 2011)

Context: New Zealand, Oceania, is an island country in the South Pacific Ocean, southeast of Australia. Located midway between the Equator and

South Pole it is made up of two main areas of landmass—North Island (115,000 square km, 71,415 square miles) and South Island. These are supplemented also by multiple smaller islands. There are 15,134 km of varied coastline and a temperate climate with regional contrasts including higher than average rainfall. Summer time falls between December and February. Although geographically covering a smaller landmass, North Island is home to a greater population (3.5 million) than South Island (1 million). Overall, 90% of the population live in the urban environment with 7.4% claiming Maori descent. The capital, Wellington, is located at the south end of the North Island with a population of around 391,000.

Geographical features include subtropical features (the northern part of the North Island), the volcanic plateau and thermal pools (North Island), glacier-fed lakes, and the Southern Alps (South Island). The predominantly mountainous terrain, coupled with the geographical isolation of the islands presents particular challenges to the flora and fauna ecosystems: 80% of plants and 25% of marine life exist in no other location. Earthquakes, volcanic activity, deforestation, soil erosion, and invasive species all present particular threats to the ecosystem. Governed by a parliamentary system and constitutional monarchy, the administrative divisions include 16 regions and 1 territory. New Zealand operates a mixed, free-market economy, with a sizeable manufacturing (24.6% of GDP) and service (70.6% of GDP) industries base, complemented by a smaller agricultural sector (4.8% of GDP).

Threat to the Urban Service System

This case study documents a disaster which played out in two parts, the first part having important consequences for the second part.

The first part occurred in the early hours of the morning (4.35 a.m. local time) of 4th September 2010; an earthquake struck New Zealand, the epicenter 55 km (35 miles) northwest of Christchurch (population approximately 386,000). It reached a magnitude of 7.0 on the Richter scale and a depth of 12 km (7.5 miles). This earthquake led to a new 11-foot wide fault line opening. It was followed by a further major earthquake on 22nd February 2011 (part two). Whilst this second earthquake reached a magnitude of only 6.3, the consequences proved to be far more devastating than the first earthquake. They also extended beyond the mainland: as a result of the shifting tectonic plates, 30 million tonnes of ice were broken off New Zealand's biggest glacier, the Tasman, causing a tsunami with waves of up to 12 feet.

The earthquake which struck New Zealand on the 4th September 2010 had only limited direct consequences: only two major injuries were reported, falling masonry and glass blamed for those affected. Why were so few affected by such a strong earthquake? Many reports claim that it was down to timing: it hit at a time when the majority of the population were asleep. Unfortunately the second earthquake was to prove far more fatal. It struck, without warning, on 22nd February 2011 at 12.51 p.m. local time. This was during a busy lunchtime, a time when the resident, and tourist, population were on the move. It was felt as far north as Wellington and was followed by two severe aftershocks, reaching magnitudes of 5.6 and 5.5 respectively. These aftershocks hit within 2 hours affecting already unstable buildings. The earthquake epicenter was placed as under the harbor at a town called Lyttelton, some 7 miles from Christchurch. Lyttelton is a tourist town, attractive for its architecture. As in Christchurch, many office workers and tourists lost in the town were out enjoying lunch.

Initial reports indicated fatalities to be in the region of 38 people, a number expected to rise to 200. By the next day these numbers had been revised to 75 fatalities, with 300 people missing. The death toll had reached 145 by the 27th February 2011 with 500 buildings damaged, including the Rugby World Cup stadium. A third of the entire building stock was placed under threat of demolition. Many people were killed by falling debris, crushed in buses and cars. Two sites proved to be particularly fatal locations: Canterbury Cathedral and Canterbury television studio. At the cathedral, the spire was displaced, windows shattered and parts of the masonry reduced to rubble. Alongside residents, a number of tourists were caught up in the disaster, many working in Christchurch as part of an extended around the world trip. The Canterbury television building was completely demolished and the scene of a particularly large number of fatalities which extended beyond the New Zealand population. The Chinese Embassy estimated a loss of 20 citizens in the building collapse, and the Japanese Embassy 10 citizens.

Types of Disruption

In this case study all the core systems (described by Dirks et al.) of transport services, local government/public services, education services, health services, and utility services received attention in media reports.

Transport Services

Whilst the first earthquake had limited consequences for transport services, the force and timing of the second earthquake resulted in considerable damage. Multiple roads were fractured making them unstable and impassable by individual car, or bus. Roads not directly affected were littered with falling masonry and building debris. Traffic lights failed to work. Bridges were destroyed. Airports (including Christchurch International Airport) and airspace were closed, initially as a precaution, whilst the quality and stability of runways were checked. TransAlpine and Transcoastal rail services were cancelled further cutting off communities already geographically isolated.

Local Government/Public Services

The public sector played a pivotal role in the immediate aftermath of the earthquake. The mayor of Christchurch, Bob Parker, a central figure in the response to both earthquakes, declared a state of emergency 4 hours after the first earthquake in 2010, prioritizing "people" in the relief efforts. Search and rescue teams were deployed, portable toilets provided, and tanks of fresh water placed around the city. The army was also sent in to manage isolated incidents of civil unrest, particularly linked to instances of looting. Animal welfare became a problem as people broke cordons to go in search of their pets. Fearing the likelihood, and consequences, of aftershocks, engineering teams were deployed to assess damage to central areas.

The response time to the second earthquake was halved: within 2 hours of the earthquake a full emergency management structure was put into place, coordinated nationally by the National Crisis Management Centre located in a bunker in the Parliament Building, the "Beehive" in Wellington. A regional emergency operations command post was established at Christchurch Art Gallery, and on the 23rd February 2011 a state of emergency was declared. Even with this state of preparedness, the authorities in Christchurch still struggled to cope in the earthquake aftermath. With heavy rains, the authorities marshaled refugees into school buildings, warehouses, and other shelters. Hundreds of people were forced to sleep head-to-toe on flower tables in a makeshift shelter in the Botanic Gardens. The public sector coordinated the recovery of fatalities, covering bodies with blankets and donated clothing whilst awaiting removal. Prioritizing the local community at the center of their relief effort, authorities issued pleas to travelers to avoid non-essential travel and avoid visiting Christchurch to allow the city to focus upon the needs of the resident population and maximize the possible success of rescue efforts.

Education Services

In spite of the drills introduced into the compulsory education sector in anticipation of possible earthquakes, the consequences of the second earthquake were extensive. The buildings simply could not withstand the intensity of the tremors. Canterbury University was closed, partially reopening over a month later with lectures taking place in tents and marquees. One hundred and sixty-three primary and secondary schools were affected, all initially closing for 3 weeks. Following this period, 90 schools were given clearance to reopen, 24 needed further assessment, and the damage at 11 sites rendered them beyond immediate repair.

Health Services

From the immediate aftermath of the second earthquake onwards, local hospitals operating in the most affected areas were inundated with casualties. These included people directly struck by falling debris, people retrieved from the rubble under buildings, and also 10 people admitted to hospital with suspected heart attacks triggered by the shock. Reports of minor injuries sustained and the effects of trauma dominated media reports at this point. Media coverage shifted in focus in the days that followed with potential health risks taking a more dominant role. Fractured sewerage pipes prompted calls for residents to boil drinking water.

Instructions to avoid flushing toilets were issued as concern arose over whether this might further contaminate the sewerage system. Elective surgeries were cancelled and patients moved around to optimize hospital space. The threat of waterborne infections increased in Christchurch as a thick sludge arising from the sand and silt foundations, a foot deep in places, covered parts of the city.

Utility Services

The second earthquake severely restricted the ability of power companies to maintain operations. Some media reports indicate that in the immediate aftermath of the February earthquake, 80% of Christchurch homes and businesses lost power and water, with utility companies struggling to rectify the situation. These power outages were not restricted to the immediate locality, but reportedly affected populations 360 km (223 miles) to the southwest of the epicenter. Whilst problematic in itself, it is important to also recognize the wider consequences of these outages—they forced hospitals to run on generator power and prompted fireman to struggle to control blazes as burst water mains reduced water pressure, with some areas out of water altogether. Power outages also led to the failure of telephone networks as mobile phone towers were forced to run on batteries with a lifespan of only a matter of hours. Communication links were in turn reduced. Power outages were compounded as temperatures dipped at night placing further strain upon compromised sources.

Types of Response

Citizen Responses

In the turmoil which followed the second earthquake, media reports document the extraordinary lengths the civilian population went to help each other. The sense of national bonding, as in previous case studies, was a uniting feature throughout. This bonding was illustrated through reports of:

1. civilians digging through the rubble with bare hands to reach others who might be trapped;

2. workmates and colleagues making stretchers from rugs or bits of debris to move the injured out from underneath collapsed masonry;
3. the use of private vehicles to get people to hospital;
4. rescuers using helicopters to pick people up from roof tops;
5. firemen using construction cranes to access trapped civilians;
6. civilians carrying the injured on makeshift stretchers to city parks where impromptu health centers were set up;
7. civilians, from opposite ends of the country, ringing to offer holiday homes and free food.

Stories of individual bravery included:

1. John Hayes, a financial accountant who used his skills from mountain climbing to save 14 colleagues by tying ropes to workers and getting them to abseil 66 feet to a car park below;
2. an Irish hero who helped people out of rubble and diverted them away from areas of leaking gas;
3. a British builder who overcame a fear of claustrophobia and worked for 12 hours pulling people to safety.

As in the previous case studies, tourists to the area were overwhelmed by offers of help from the local population regarding transport and accommodation.

The intensity of the earthquake also generated considerable fear within the local community, many expressing a desire to leave, if they had not already done so. A rise in domestic violence was reported as thousands were left homeless and feared further earthquakes. People used technology to keep abreast of the unfolding disaster: "My laptop was still connected to Facebook and friends in New Zealand were feeding me information (...) I could hear breaking glass and screaming all around me. It was bizarre—I was getting information live from New Zealand."[8] A Japanese teacher managed to send an e-mail home to his family while trapped in the rubble of a school. Technology was also used by people to text messages to communicate for a final time with their loved ones, and to call for help: "Mummy I got buried [in the Christchurch rubble].

Please make it quick."[9] Tales of desperate communications such as these illustrate the deep emotional and psychological anguish disasters on this scale can generate.

Local Government/Public Services Responses

In the immediate aftermath of the second earthquake, the rescue and response fell primarily to ordinary citizens and emergency services on duty. Within 2 hours a full emergency management structure was in place, under the coordination of the National Crisis Management Centre operating from a bunker in the Beehive in Wellington. Civil Defense assumed the role of lead agency. Canterbury District Health Board coordinated health and medical support across the city. Elective surgery was cancelled and patients were moved to increase capacity. Donations of generators and free calls were made. Water was rationed and provided via milk tankers and bottled supplies. More than 2,000 portaloos, 5,000 chemical toilets, portable shower units, extra flights, medical supplies, and hot meals were made available. Temporary accommodation was set up in local schools for displaced residents. The education sector was hit, with learning hubs established to provide student support, particularly for those of a secondary school age, to work at home whilst repairs were ongoing.

There was a substantial emergency services and military response to the second earthquake with all army medical staff mobilized, alongside several hundred troops. Emergency services, operating through an emergency regional operations command center housed in the city's new art gallery, performed multiple amputations to free trapped survivors, responded to texts and tapping sounds from the living, and utilized DNA and fingerprints to identify fatalities. These services were supported by Australian doctors who were in Christchurch attending a conference at the time of the second earthquake. Tents were provided in parks on the outskirts of the city at nightfall whilst the center of Christchurch was evacuated with only emergency services allowed in. The army performed multiple tasks including operating desalination plants to provide water, and setting up military roadblocks around the city center after a curfew was imposed following outbreaks of looting.

This response was supported by a substantial international relief effort:

1. Australia sent a Hercules aircraft with 40 rescue specialists on board. In addition, 300 Australian police were sworn in as New Zealand Police to perform regular duties and "reassurance patrols," to man police security cordons, to organize evacuations, to assist with search and rescue operations, to liaise with families over missing persons, to support media briefings and tours of the affected areas, to collect forensic data, and to assist with traffic and looting control.

2. The British Foreign Office sent a team of 62 emergency workers from England and Wales.

3. In order to provide satellite imagery for rescue operations, French and American civil protection agencies requested the activation of the International Charter on Space and Major Disasters.

4. Search and rescue teams were deployed from Japan, Australia, the United Kingdom, the United States of America, Taiwan, China, and Singapore.

5. A team of fire fighters from Grampian, Scotland were put on standby to fly out to help the rescue effort.

Business Responses

Following the first earthquake, by Monday September 6th 2010, 2 days after the event, power companies had returned power to 90% of Christchurch and water supplies had resumed for all but 15%–20% of residents. Following the second earthquake, businesses introduced innovative ways of supporting the relief effort. Google established a "person finder" application for their systems. Designed to allow families and friends of the missing to post information, the uptake of the application was instant with 3,600 entries of people who were safe posted in the first few days after the disaster. In an act of goodwill, mobile phone companies scrapped charges and airlines flew people at a fraction of the usual cost. A number of business people made individual donations to help the residents, with one entrepreneur giving £1.8million toward the reconstruction of Christchurch Cathedral. In contrast, Lloyd's of London insurers anticipated losses in the region of billions, blaming the earthquake and Australian floods for their poor performance.

Third Sector Responses

Raising money to support disaster victims and the region more generally generated a considerable amount of media coverage with celebrities once again dominating the literature. Celebrities pledged support including:

1. footballer Winston Reid auctioning off football memorabilia to raise funds for the recovery effort in Christchurch;
2. Hayley Westenra, a 23-year-old singer, launching Quake Aid, a national fundraising concert at Auckland's Vector Arena.

Similar to the earlier two case studies, once again the third sector played an important role in the immediate medical response to the crisis. St John Ambulance coordinated triage stations at medical emergency posts, whilst the New Zealand Red Cross and Salvation Army provided humanitarian and welfare support.

Summary

This chapter has provided us with background details on three distinct case studies of unsettled times: the floods in Queensland Australia (2010 and 2011); the Japanese earthquake and tsunami which hit Japan in 2011; and the earthquakes which hit Christchurch, New Zealand in September 2010 and February 2011. In each case study we have explored the types of disruption occurring and outlined the broad range of responses evident in each of the urban service systems examined. Regardless of the reason for unsettled times, each case study has provided us with examples of citizens who have temporarily fallen below the level of consumption adequacy. They have illustrated the short-term, and in some cases, longer-term consequences of these changing circumstances. In the next chapter we use the case study material to tackle questions linked to impact and likelihood. These questions are designed to help us to make sense of what happens to urban service systems when they are faced with unsettled times.

Review and Discussion Questions

1. What does the term "natural disasters" refer to?
2. Which "core system" gains the least media attention in each of the case studies? Why might this be the case?
3. Looking across the three case studies, which common approaches were employed by the third sector in their response to unsettled times?
4. What evidence is there that the impact of unsettled times was felt beyond the immediate geographical location?
5. Based upon the experiences outlined in the three case studies, in what ways might information technology, e.g., social media, be better utilized in future disaster management plans?

CHAPTER 6

Impact, Likelihood, and Resilience

Analyzing Service System Responses to Unsettled Times

Introduction

In the previous chapter, using national media datasets, we reported three case study examples of unsettled times. The types of disruption generated and responses arising were considered on an individual case study basis, at a macro- and meso-level. These case studies were chosen to exemplify the unsettled times which might arise as a consequence of environmental and climatic conditions; conditions which we indicated in Chapter 1 are central to this book. Climatic conditions are a particularly important contributor to unsettled times. During the period 1980–2007, they accounted for 98% of all natural disasters. On average, over 375 million people per year are affected by climate-related disasters. Over 2 million people have been killed by natural disasters since 1975. This is forecast to increase 54% by 2015.[1]

In this chapter, we analyze what happens to urban service systems when they are severely compromised by unsettled times. We question which parts of the service system become particularly vulnerable during these circumstances, and why. We use the relative impact and relative likelihood framework outlined in Chapter 1 to question the extent to which the service systems central to our case studies are resilient to change. In doing so, we provide insights into the salient issues which citizens, and service systems, face during unsettled times. These insights also have implications for consumption adequacy, causing citizens, albeit at times only temporarily, to fall below levels of consumption adequacy. Our focus in this chapter is upon the service system rather than the individual.

Impact

In Chapter 1, we defined impact in three ways: spatial scope; functional scope; and temporal scope (see Figure 6.1).

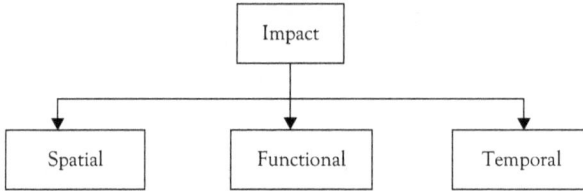

Figure 6.1. Scope of impact.

Spatial Scope

By *spatial scope* we are considering the extent to which the impact of unsettled times is geographically confined, be it to an administrative/governmental jurisdictional area, or whether the impact is felt more widely across such boundaries.

In the Australian case study, there are multiple examples of citizens dispersed over a wide geographical region who were directly affected by the floods. On the 30th December 2010, 1,000 people were evacuated in Queensland and 300 people living in the town of Theodore relocated as a direct consequence of the floods. By the 3rd January 2011, floods had devastated 22 cities and towns across Queensland, including the tourist town of Rockhampton. On the 10th January 2011, an inland tsunami hit the town of Toowoomba with 12 people declared dead and 72 identified as missing. Residents of Australia's third largest city, Brisbane, were warned to prepare for the worst floods in more than a century whilst the entire population of Forest Hill (300 people) were airlifted to safety. By the 2nd February 2011, a 190-mile stretch of coastline had been put on alert and floodwaters were reported to be engulfing Grantham.

In the Japanese case study, a similar pattern of spatial impact can be observed, although this time with an extra twist, the potential for a nuclear disaster. On the 11th March 2011, the earthquake of 9.0 magnitude triggered a 15–20 m high tsunami which travelled 6 miles inland affecting multiple communities across a wide geographical area. Multiple nuclear power plants are located within this area. The disaster prompted a loss of power across Japan, with the nuclear power plant at Fukushima directly affected. The loss of power resulted in the overheating of the Fukushima reactor core, and a dangerous build-up of gases. Japanese armed forces and U.S. Air Force pilots were scrambled to deliver a specialist coolant to the stricken reactor. Pressure levels reached 1.5 times the normal level. The threat was not limited to Fukushima however, but spatially spread across a number of other geographical regions. The Ongagawa nuclear plant, 80 miles north of Fukushima, for instance experienced a fire in the turbine hall but this was safely distinguished with no radiation leakages. Media reports also indicated the precautionary shutdown of a further five nuclear plants dispersed across Japan.

The New Zealand case study presents a slightly different set of spatial circumstances to consider. On the 4th September 2010, the first earthquake which struck at 4.35 a.m. local time had an epicenter 55 km (35 miles) northwest of Christchurch. This earthquake is spatially interesting as it led to a new 11-foot wide fault line opening, and, in effect, a new subterranean map of the region being drawn. The second earthquake which struck on the 22nd February 2011 had a much greater direct impact upon the population, striking at 12.51 p.m. local time, during a busy lunchtime period. This time whilst the damage was largely contained within the Christchurch region, Lyttelton, the town at the epicenter of the earthquake, some 7 miles away, other communities outside this region were also affected, albeit to a lesser degree, with power outages linked to the earthquake reported some 360 km (223 miles) away.

Functional Scope

By *functional scope* we are questioning the extent to which the impact of unsettled times is restricted to one, or certain parts of the service system. By this we mean:

1. Is the impact felt only within the transportation sector, or the health sector, for instance?
2. Does it cover multiple parts of the system?
3. Is the impact evenly spread across each of the functions of the system?

The core systems identified by Dirks et al. (transport services; local government/public services; health services; utility services) are central to this analysis as these are the systems which allow citizens to function.

They assist in determining the extent to which levels of consumption adequacy are upheld during unsettled times.

Whether we consider the case studies separately, or collectively, it is very apparent that each disaster resulted in widespread functional disruption to each of the service systems in question with multiple parts of the system affected. Examples of disruption include reports detailing:

1. the destruction of homes, offices, shops, and other buildings;
2. falling masonry and glass;
3. panic buying of foodstuff;
4. power outages, a lack of water, fuel, food, and sanitation;
5. severe damage to transportation and communications infrastructure (e.g., road blockages and precautionary airport closures);
6. the displacement of many residents, including tourists.

Service system failures unique to each case study also emerged. In the Australian example, the inability of the flood defenses to cope with excessive flooding led to mass evacuations on a scale previously unseen. In the Japanese example, the overwhelming nature of the disaster led to a communications systems (e.g., telephone) overload. In the case of New Zealand, breakdowns in the service system also generated fears of civil unrest, particularly looting.

None of these functional disruptions occurred in isolation, however. The more common functional disruptions had what might be termed a "ripple effect." Residents were displaced *because of* building collapses or utility service failures. Business output fell *because* roads were blocked and airports closed for precautionary reasons. Nothing happened in isolation. As such, these patterns of disruption highlight the interconnectedness of service systems and the fact that these systems are highly complex, themselves representing, in effect, a "system of systems."

Temporal Scope

By *temporal scope* we are referring to the duration of unsettled times:

1. Is the impact limited to only a short-term time period?
2. Is it likely to cover an extended time period?

As the discussion will show, these events do indeed have both short- and longer-term consequences which need to be built in to developing contingency plans for system resilience.

In two of the case studies, the floods in Australia and the earthquake/tsunami in Japan, the direct temporal scope of the disaster was largely limited to a 3-month period. In the New Zealand case study, the direct temporal scope extended over a 7-month period, with the majority of the activity, and consequences, felt in the final two months. However the consequences of each disaster extended well beyond the initial impact as a review of the Japanese case study highlights.

As a result of the disaster, Japan experienced its first trade deficit in 31 years as the nuclear problems at Fukushima raised dependence on imported fuels. Fukushima previously accounted for 29% of electricity generated, a figure that had been expected to rise to 50% by 2030. Confidence fell in the international luxury goods market associated with Japan. Even before concerns arose over the nuclear threat, the luxury goods index had fallen by 4%. Burberry, with 7% of its sales in Japan, lost 6% of its value. The commodity markets of rice, copper, oil, and sugar were threatened. Businesses struggled to trade, some disappearing entirely: one soy sauce maker lost his entire 200-year old family business and 70% of his client base. Insurers were faced with a $15 billion bill globally prompting them to issue a string of profit warnings. Trading on the world stock market was extremely volatile with initial news of the earthquake promoting a sharp share drop in price and sell off across Asian stock markets affecting the economic stability of the country. To prop up the Japanese economy, the G7 group of industrialized nations intervened in the foreign exchange market selling 22 billion yen in a coordinated activity.

Likelihood

In Chapter 1, we defined likelihood in two ways: propensity and preparedness (see Figure 6.2).

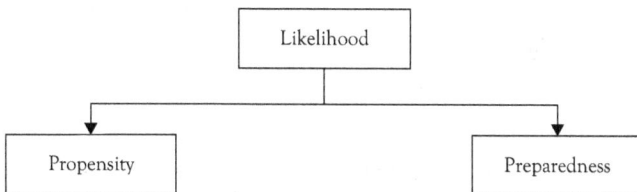

Figure 6.2. Likelihood.

Propensity

By propensity we are referring to how inclined, or predisposed, an area is to experience particular types of unsettled times. Here we consider questions related to:

1. Is it a one-off isolated event?
2. Is it likely to recur?
3. Is it linked to seasonality, or the geographical location, geological makeup, or both of the region?

Floods in Australia, and the Queensland area more particularly, are common. Indeed severe flooding in 1974 in Brisbane led to the development of the Wivenhoe Dam, a flood mitigation and water storage dam built upstream across the Brisbane River. Abnormal weather conditions have occurred periodically since then. For the towns of Rockhampton, a tourism center 350 miles north of Brisbane, Toowoomba, Forest Hill and Australia's third largest city Brisbane, the likelihood of flooding was known for a considerable period of time. The events of January and February 2011 actually began to gather momentum 6 months earlier and in an entirely different geographical location. As early as June 2010, meteorologists mapping weather hazards linked to La Nina, a phenomenon characterized by the extensive cooling of the central and eastern tropical Pacific Ocean, observed freak conditions with the potential to result in severe flooding. Yet, even given the apparent high propensity for such events, the climate-related events of late 2010 and early 2011 still took the area by apparent surprise: "It's 2011 and we've never been so vulnerable; we try to tame it, but yet again Australia has been struck by the shocking force of Nature."[2]

Similarly, natural hazards are common in Japan. The geography of the landscape, which includes dormant and active volcanic activity (with approximately 1,500 seismic occurrences annually), tsunami, and typhoons, has resulted in the area being named the "ring of fire." Earthquakes are more frequent than volcanic eruptions, even though approximately one-third of Japan's 186 volcanoes are active. Yet even given the high propensity for these hazards to occur, the earthquake, tsunami, and aftershocks took this region by surprise. The magnitude resulted in a high death toll and fears of a nuclear disaster, a secondary consequence of the tsunami. It also accentuated the potential for man-made hazards, particularly linked to nuclear power plants.

New Zealand is also an area with a high propensity or disposition toward earthquakes. The region lies on two tectonic plates. Consequently, earthquakes are a common occurrence. The area experiences more than 14,000 earthquakes a year, of which only about 150 are felt and around 20 are in excess of 5.0 in magnitude. Prior to the 4th September 2010, the last major earthquake took place in South Island in July 2009. This earthquake reached a magnitude of 7.8 and reportedly moved the southern tip of New Zealand 12 inches closer to Australia, redrawing both the surface and subterranean maps. As each of our case studies confirms, these are not one-off isolated events. Each region has experienced similar events before, albeit not necessarily on the same scale. Their geographical location, and geological and climatological makeup place them at a high propensity to experience similar events again.

Preparedness

By preparedness we are referring to how well-organized an area is to respond to unsettled times. In this section, we consider the extent to which service systems have been designed to anticipate or plan for possible unsettled times. We also question whether plans developed extend throughout the entire service system design.

In the Australian case study, the opportunities for preparedness were high: the likelihood of a disaster was high and known for 6 months. However, even with the evidence available and warnings issued, many reports suggest that some parts of the service system of Queensland were ill-prepared to resist the disaster that followed. Utility services took a particular hit with power systems experiencing overload, and flood defenses breached. Other parts of the service system were better prepared for the disaster. From the beginning of the crisis, in December 2010, forced evacuations were put into place across all the towns and cities most affected. These evacuations were conducted both for safety reasons, and also to clear the area to allow personnel, police, and essential services to search for missing persons. Public services provided citizens with instructions on what to take with them to evacuation centers: torches, matches, radios, medication, birth and marriage certificates, and previous photographs all on the list. Citizens were directed to emergency shelters with the expectation of a 1-week long stay.

Prior to 2010, the last fatal earthquake in the Christchurch area took place some 40 years earlier in 1968 killing three people. Given the time lapse between disasters, and the differing geographical landscape of New Zealand, it could be argued that the state of preparedness might be less than the Japanese case study. Yet interestingly, New Zealand did exhibit signs of anticipation, even given the time lag between disasters. The media reports outlined the preventative actions introduced by government services in anticipation of a possible threat. These actions included a rolling program of tough building regulations ensuring that high rise blocks were designed to sway not shake, that building foundations were loaded with rubber and steel shock absorbers, and joints were reinforced. Additionally, the introduction of regular earthquake drills from primary school upwards was designed to instill a confidence within the community that they could take a degree of control when faced with emergent disasters.

Of all the case studies Japan was, in theory, the most prepared for unsettled times. The region experiences multiple earthquakes, on a regular basis. School children, and citizens more generally, are regularly drilled in how to react when warning alarms sound. As the words of Taiko Sawadate, a 59-year-old nurse from Otsuchi City, illustrate: "When the alarm bell rang I had about 20 minutes to evacuate with my mother. We drove even higher than the recommended safe area, so I was sure it was OK."[3] The population is well versed in potential disasters. The speed of the response to the earthquake and tsunami, the immediate declaration of a state of emergency, and the short-term disruption to communication networks all provide indications of a system designed with resilience in mind. However, this case study also exposes an additional factor to take into account when designing resilient service systems, namely what to do in the event of a double disaster. Service systems were in place to respond to an earthquake. Yet the location of a number of evacuation centers along coastal areas suggests Japan was less prepared for a tsunami, even given the high propensity for an earthquake to move tectonic plates, which in turn might result in a tsunami. Thinking beyond the single "type" of unsettled times and building a system which anticipates multiple threats is the lesson that emerges from this case study.

Resilience

Earlier in our work (Chapters 1 and 4), we introduced the concept of urban service system resilience, that is, the ability of a system to anticipate, absorb, and adapt to, recover, or both from a disruptive event. In assessing how resilient the service systems in our case studies are, we return now to the four principal strategic components central to an assessment of resilience:

1. Resistance
2. Reliability
3. Redundancy
4. Response and recovery

Resistance

This strategic component focuses upon the prevention of damage or disruption to a system through design factors. Each of our case studies includes evidence of service systems developed in part to resist unsettled times: buildings strengthened; flood defenses built, for instance. Yet each case study also provides us with evidence of service system failures: collapsing buildings; breached flood defenses. Both the Australian and New Zealand case studies provide us with some insights into why resistance strategies can fall short in unsettled times. They both illustrate the need for service system design to be an integral part of a wider environmental and planning policy.

In the Australian example, there are fundamental differences of opinion evident in what represents the most likely threat to the Australian region. The "warmists lobby" suggests droughts to be the primary concern, when floods were the reality. Second, agricultural policy and the clearing of forests leading to a change of the ecosystem are frequently blamed as creating unsettled times. Third, whilst an early warning system was in place, people chose to ignore alarm systems when activated and to instead defend their property. Fourth, the poor quality of available data and limited scientific understanding inevitably compromise the ability of service systems to respond.

In the New Zealand example, resistance to the second earthquake was compromised by multiple factors including:

1. location—this earthquake struck close to a city center with a large resident population;
2. depth—the epicenter was four times closer to ground level than previous earthquakes;
3. timing—it took place during the middle of the day, at a time when an increased number of people would have been on the move enjoying lunch;
4. robustness of the buildings—in spite of being constructed in anticipation of earthquakes, many building structures were weakened by the earlier September 2010 earthquake and the 4,000 aftershocks linked to it;
5. geology of the disaster—the City of Christchurch is built on an alluvial plain, on sediments that are vulnerable to transforming into a liquid when shaken. This process, referred to as liquefaction, causes the ground to lose rigidity.

Reliability

This strategic component focuses upon the need to design systems capable of operating under a range of conditions. Of the three case studies it is the Japanese example which provides the most evidence of system resilience: a major highway running through the Tohoku region, at the heart of the disaster, reopened after only 2 weeks; the bullet train, the Shinkansen, linking Tokyo and the Tohoku region reopened within 6 weeks. This case study also aptly illustrates though that resilience may only be linked to one part of the service system. Whilst the transport and communications system were planned and managed to withstand the impact of the disaster, residential accommodation was less reliable with some reports indicating that even 3 months post the initial disaster, 124,000 residents were still living in evacuation centers.

In tackling the issue of service system design and contingency planning there are also multiple longer-term ongoing consequences of which we need to take account. For instance, in the Australian case example, the mining and agricultural industries were hit the hardest with billions lost in delays and lost production. The floods shut down the mining operations of the Rio Tinto Group forcing them to declare force majeure. This is a legal clause which is included in contracts to mitigate the obligations of an organization to honor their contractual obligations during natural and unavoidable catastrophes. The mining industry lost in the order of A$100 million a day with the consequences of these actions extending beyond the immediate short term. They led to a hike in coal prices, rising to a 2-year high, and the panic buying of fuel. Insurance companies, anticipating substantial claims, increased their premiums. The export of coal, wheat, and sugar was also affected by the floods. In turn, this led to price increases in associated fuel and foodstuff, bread, for instance.

Redundancy

This strategic component is concerned with the availability of backup installations and spare capacity. Of the four components this is the weakest area of system resilience. For instance, in the Australian case study utility services took two particular hits during these unsettled times. First, in anticipation of a pending flood, companies cut power supplies to likely affected areas on safety grounds. This was widely reported to be the case in Queensland, where even large areas of the Brisbane city center had their power supplies cut off for protective reasons. Additionally however, the surge of floodwaters in Rockhampton, Brisbane, and Toowoomba took the authorities off guard and led to the severe unplanned disruption of power supplies with 4,000 homes losing power entirely. Backup supplies failed. Spare capacity was not available. Similar instances were reported in the other two case studies with telecommunications networks coming under particular criticism for failing network coverage and overloaded networks.

Response and Recovery

This strategic component focuses upon the need for service systems to recover fast and effectively when compromised. As we can see, widespread spatial disruption was felt in each of the case studies. It was not contained within any one administrative area, but rather spread across multiple areas, each with their own administrative bodies and particular circumstances. This has quite extensive implications for the response and recovery of a region to unsettled times as it increases the opportunities for efforts to be duplicated and information to be reinterpreted or even misinterpreted. Indeed the limited reporting of the coordination of relief efforts in any of the case studies did indicate instances where efforts were duplicated. This was further compounded by the fact that the range of spatial impact and circumstances was by no means uniform. The Australian example covers the widest geographical area with multiple authorities and types of environment affected. Compare this to the New Zealand example which was, on the surface, the most spatially contained, yet still covered a number of administrative regions. The more spatially diverse the situation, the greater is the potential for a lack of coordinated effort.

Response and recovery is also affected by functional factors. One feature of functional disruption is that different functions are affected in different ways. The education function for instance, in contrast to the other core elements, received relatively little coverage within media reports. Where it did appear it was usually to comment on the preparatory drills taking place in schools prior to incidents of unsettled times. This introduces another distinction to our understanding of service system failures: as well as being relative to particular circumstances, these failures might also be differentiated as direct or indirect. By direct we mean these are the problems immediately arising, most salient, and at the epicenter of unsettled times. Breakdowns in transportation, communications, and utility services are salient to each case study. They were the problems most immediately and acutely felt. They directly compromised the ability of citizens, at both an individual and collective level, to function. Indirect impacts are those which emerge on the periphery. They are less acute in the immediate aftermath of a disaster, yet they remain, or even grow, in significance over time. The impact of education provision is an important example here.

Summary

In this chapter, we have used the relative impact (spatial, functional, and temporal) and the relative likelihood (propensity and preparedness) framework to extend our understanding of the resilience of service systems in our three case study regions. From this analysis we can conclude that spatial impact might be both above ground and also subterranean. It is most common for this impact to cross administrative boundaries multiplying the opportunities for misunderstanding and duplication of effort. Multiple functions of the service system are usually affected in unsettled times, although different functions are ordinarily affected to different degrees. The interconnectedness of service systems does generate what we term the "ripple effect" and increase the chances of systems failure. These failures are not uniform across the system with preparatory actions most common across the transport and communications system. These failures in turn lead to citizens falling below levels of consumption adequacy, albeit temporarily in most instances. Our case study analysis thus far has allowed us to consider the macro- and meso-level of impact and likelihood. In Chapter 7, we move on to a detailed analysis of a UK-based case study and, in doing so, extend our understanding of factors which may affect service systems in the micro-environment.

Review and Discussion Questions

1. In each case study, to what extent was the spatial scope of unsettled times geographically confined?
2. In each case study, to what extent was the impact of unsettled times restricted to one function of the service system?
3. Which examples of short- and longer-term impact were evident in each case study?
4. Which case study has a high propensity to experience similar events again? And why?
5. If you were to map the four strategic components of resilience onto the three case studies, how would each case study perform?

CHAPTER 7

Unsettled Times

The Case of the UK "Big Freeze" of 2010

Introduction

In Chapter 5, three case studies illustrated how different forms of disasters and complex emergencies create unsettled times for communities. The case studies also demonstrate (in Chapter 6) that variations can occur depending on impact (functional, temporal, and spatial) and likelihood (which involves the degree of preparedness and anticipation). In this chapter, we have chosen a case study brought about by out-of-the-ordinary weather conditions for the particular location. The impact is low, if measured by the number of deaths, and the effects cover a relatively short period of time in comparison to the cases covered in Chapter 5. There are some interesting features relating to anticipation and preparedness, and the unsettled times affected a wide range of functions in the whole of the United Kingdom. The case study concerns occurrences of the "big freeze" that hit the United Kingdom at both the beginning and end of 2010.

This case study has been chosen for a more comprehensive analysis because:

1. the authors have access to detailed accounts of the effects of the "big freeze" through both local and national news stories. This affords the opportunity to delve beneath the headlines, and envisage the world of the citizens during the period of unsettled times;
2. this, in turn, provides the basis for understanding the service ecosystem, and the multiple actors and interactions that may remain latent under normal weather conditions;
3. it represents an occurrence that has happened several times before, but one which always seems to find traditional service providers,

including public services, unprepared. This lack of preparedness is, in part, the reason why many citizens temporarily fall below the level of consumption adequacy;

4. there are lessons to be learned from studying the case study through the lenses of service science and the service-dominant logic (SDL) of marketing.

Background to the Case Study

Winter in the United Kingdom consists of the months of December, January, and February. For example, the temperatures on *average* in London vary between 4°C and 8°C in December, and between 2°C and 7°C in January and February. They are slightly lower in northern parts of the United Kingdom. Of course, average figures do not tell the whole story, and variations can be large, especially at the lower end. Extreme cold— "big freezes"—can occur. They occur relatively infrequently: the last three big freezes occurred in 1947, 1962/3, and 2010. When they do occur, however, they contribute significantly to unsettled times for UK citizens. There are many places on the globe where winter temperatures are as low, or even lower, than those experienced in the UK big freezes, but they happen every year and so their populations are prepared, and seem to cope much better. In this case study, we focus on the 2010 big freeze, but start with comparisons with 1947 and 1962/3 to illustrate the apparent, continuing lack of ability of UK service infrastructure and service systems to cope with disruptions caused by extreme winter conditions.

Big Freezes Compared

Below are selections of news items relating the big freezes of 1947, 1962/3, and 2010. Five have been taken from each and randomly presented. See if you can tell which time period the items are from. There are clues, but it is not easy.

1. "The next 12 days or so were the height of the crisis, with the weather unremittingly grim and unemployment rising to over 1.75 million (compared to just over 400,000 in mid-January)."

2. "Domestic cuts meant no electricity between the hours of 9.00 am to 12 noon."

3. "Shared adversity has brought out a public spirit that has seen people take hot food to elderly neighbors, and parents and children shovelling snow from school playgrounds."

4. "A number of international airlines are thought to be seeking compensation because of the snow chaos, with analysts estimating that the total cost to airlines was more than £100 million."

5. "It was clear that many old people were suffering severe hardship as a result of shortage of fuel."

6. "The road salting was becoming ineffective. Temperatures were so low that even salt water froze."

7. "Some midwives used tractors to reach isolated communities in the worst-affected areas."

8. "More than 1,000 schools were closed yesterday in Scotland, Wales and Northern Ireland."

9. "Public transport simply could not run, and, with whole villages cut off for days, the RAF was forced to make food drops to the stranded populace."

10. "Road and rail transport was severely disrupted, the airports closed and the Thames froze over."

11. "Children returning to school were sent home as the heating was not working and threats of power cuts due to industrial action by power workers was on the cards."

12. "Almost 100 factories had their gas supplies cut off yesterday to ensure that there was enough power to meet soaring residential demand."

13. "In Surrey and Middlesex, millions of commuters stayed at home."

14. "Farmers could not tend their crops and livestock. Vegetables were simply frozen in the ground."

15. "Power cuts became the norm, refuse remained uncollected and people had to get water from road tankers as the mains supply froze as well."

While there is a 63-year gap between the big freezes, it is difficult to discern the differences in the news items, despite massive changes in technology and available infrastructure.[1] In each case, core services—transport, government, social services, education, public safety, health, and utilities—broke down. These are services that citizens living above the level of consumption adequacy take for granted. It can be argued, as many do, that due to the relative infrequency of big freezes, it is uneconomical to plan a satisfactory response. What is the point of stockpiling thousands of tons of rock salt or "grit," for example, when it is unlikely to be used? However, it is still remarkable that over a period that has seen so many advances in information and communication technology (ICT), citizens in the 2010 big freeze faced a similar level of unsettlement and lack of resilience to those in 1947.

The 2010 Big Freeze—A Story of Unsettled Times

The year 2010 was very unusual for the United Kingdom. Not only did abnormally cold weather disrupt the region at the beginning of the year, but also it returned at the end of the year as well. So from 5 January to the end of February 2010, and also from the 29 November until 25 December, 2010, the United Kingdom was in the grip of what became known as the "big freeze." For the purpose of this case study, we will make no distinction between the two periods in 2010, as the effect of the separate cases of abnormally low temperatures was remarkably similar.

In both cases, there were disruptions to all the core urban systems identified by Dirks et al.[2] Education services, health services, transport services, utility services, public services, and recreation services either could not cope with, or failed to respond to the big freeze. Specifically, there were car, bus, air, and rail disruptions; school closures; reduced ambulance services; issues of coping with peak gas/electricity demand for longer periods; highways/roads closed; dangerously icy pavements/sidewalks; garbage left uncollected; and sports fixtures cancelled. All UK citizens experienced severe deprivation of the many services that contribute to their well-being and this had many knock-on effects for the UK economy. In some cases, the big freeze led to death—year-on-year comparisons suggest that almost 300 people per day died from causes linked to the extreme weather. Below, based on news stories relating to the 2010 big freeze, we offer insights which give a more vivid picture of life at that time than the main headlines and statistics.

Stories of the individual affected core services will be followed by a specific example that demonstrates the extent of interconnectedness between system elements. We begin each story with typical headlines of the time.

Transport Services

Thousands stranded as airports ground many flights, trains are cancelled and motorways shut down.[3]

Ambulance chiefs have cancelled transport for non-emergency hospital appointments after the weather made side roads impassable.[4]

We are anticipating a 60% increase in breakdown calls today. The AA [Automobile Association] received more than 18,000 emergency call-outs yesterday, with the figure set to increase in the next couple of days.[5]

Road, air, and rail transport services are always affected by a big freeze and contribute to a large volume of news items.

In the United Kingdom, as in many countries, roads are graded. At the top level are motorways, normally three-lane carriageways in each direction, going for hundreds of miles, which connect major cities, or provide "ring roads" around the cities. At the next level are "A" roads, some of which are dual carriageways, and many of which provide routes through suburban areas. Below that are "B" roads, many of which are in more rural areas, and side roads and side streets which serve residential areas in towns and cities. The normal reaction to problems caused by snow and ice is to attend to highways, through road "gritting" (rock salt dropped on to the road by specially designed vehicles), in the order of the hierarchy of roads. Thus the motorways are gritted first, then the A roads, and (assuming there is any rock salt left) the B roads (especially public transport routes), and side streets. However, particularly in rural areas, snow ploughs are required to shift especially high snow drifts.

While there is a logic to a policy that aims to attend first to roads with the greatest volume of traffic, it is also obvious that many car users must negotiate B roads and side streets before getting to A roads or motorways. Also public service road transport—buses, ambulances, refuse collectors, for example—must access B roads, side roads, and remote rural areas. Further complications follow as "grit" runs out in some areas quicker than others, and cars, trucks, and buses either break down or become totally immovable, causing problems for other motorists.

When road transport systems break down, there are obvious repercussions, and some less obvious "knock-on" effects that become salient. People in the United Kingdom expect to use road transport to, for example, get to work and school, to go shopping, to visit friends and relatives, to get to medical centers and hospitals, to visit restaurants, pubs, and entertainment venues, and to link with other transport services (rail and air). Haulage firms, distribution centers, taxis, bus and ambulance services, petrol (gas) deliveries, and refuse collections all rely on the efficiency of the road transport network. It is not difficult to envisage the economic and social costs associated with the non-operation of these services. However, the dependency of UK citizens and organizations on road transport was demonstrated in many other news items:

1. The Christmas shopping activity, on which most retailers depend, was compacted into a 2-week rather than 6-week period. Even e-retailing was affected as it requires road delivery for order fulfillment.
2. Insurance claims spiraled, following accidents and rescues.
3. Mail delay of many days meant that needy families failed to receive welfare payments. Also many bills remained unpaid.
4. Driving tests were cancelled.
5. Criminal justice was on hold as courts were closed.
6. Councils lost thousands of pounds in parking revenue.
7. Winter tourism in Scotland was severely affected.

Rail services, while generally more resilient to bad weather, also were severely affected. Over the period, almost a third of trains serving the United Kingdom were cancelled. Many UK rail systems operate on what is known as the "third rail" system: this is a safety system whereby ice on the third rail will shut down trains as a protective device. The United Kingdom is the only country in the world that has a third rail system outside a rural area. Consequently, at a time where temperatures went as low as −21°C, and the mean January temperature was −2.1°C, third rail systems operated only intermittently. Coupled with frozen points failures, fuel freezing on diesel trains, and damage to trains from frozen blocks of ice bouncing upwards from tracks, this meant that many train services were being cancelled without warning. In Scotland, for example, this resulted in £500,000 of ticket refunds to maintain goodwill, and pleas for customers (with access to the Internet) to take responsibility for consulting the rail company's website before commencing their journey.

The United Kingdom's failure to handle airport and airline disruptions is a feature of the 2010 big freeze that attracted worldwide negative publicity as well as affecting the quality of life of many people who were unable to fly for business and social reasons. While in 1947 and 1962/3, such disruptions would have only affected a minority of UK citizens and travelers from overseas, in 2010, it not only affected millions of UK and other citizens, but the 24-hour news broadcasts, together with social media communication, ensured that it was widely known. The inability of UK airports to cope is well known. However, it is worth cataloging the effects and ramifications.

From a business perspective, airlines suffered huge direct losses through cancelled flights, as well as the indirect effect of negative customer perceptions and word of mouth. British Airways, for example, estimated that cancelled flights to and from London Heathrow airport cost it £50 million. British Airways, together with other airlines, sought compensation from the company operating London Heathrow Airport, British Airport Authority (BAA), which they blamed for the scale of the disruption. At the height of the disruptions, the offer by the chief executive of BAA to forgo his 2010 bonus exacerbated the dispute and added to the increasingly inept public relations surrounding air travel. Blame attribution for the chaos was taking place at the same time that thousands of air travelers were kept waiting in airports and planes with little or no information being given to them. One result was that the Salvation Army provided mobile soup kitchens at Heathrow airport, prompting the comment from a stranded passenger that, "the Salvation Army have shown more care and grace towards us than the airlines and BAA combined."[6]

Local Government/Public Services

Potholes in their thousands are emerging as the cold spell continues. Hundreds of millions of pounds will be needed to mend crumbling roads.[7]

Piles of rubbish are mounting up outside houses because refuse lorries are unable to get through. Sending 26-tonne dustcarts down icy streets, packed with cars and pedestrians was deemed dangerous.[8]

Liverpool City Council today ran out of grit after using more than 250 tonnes since December 29.[9]

Local authorities are responsible for a range of public services. The services that they seemingly cannot carry out efficiently in a big freeze are those concerned with road maintenance and rubbish (garbage) collection.

Gritting with rock salt is the main means for tackling roads made impassable through snow and ice. Each local authority will have stocks of rock salt that can cope with a normal winter. These stocks are soon depleted with a cold spell of several days below freezing. The problem is compounded by some areas of the country being affected more than others, with local supplies of rock salt completely running out. There is then a national problem, beyond the auspices of local authorities, of the logistics of using the national stock of rock salt in the most efficient way. Clearly the whole road transport system depends totally on road gritting efficiencies. The road network suffers another consequence that adds to the local authority's problems and costs. The ice and road clearing operations destroy road surfaces and create potholes that in turn damage cars and lorries that use those roads.

Normally, rubbish (garbage) is collected, once a week, from all houses in a local authority. Domestic and business rubbish bins (wheelie bins) are emptied as the council lorries go through every side road in the residential areas. Where access to the roads is prevented through snow/ice, either the bins are left unemptied and piles of rubbish accumulate in plastic bags around the bins, or residents are urged to wheel their bins to a more major road that is accessible to the lorries. Not all residents are physically capable of doing this. In some areas, rubbish remained uncollected for 5–8 weeks, and the situation was particularly bad in children's play areas around blocks of apartments.

Education Services

> Hundreds of thousands of children enjoyed an extra day off school yesterday, as icy conditions prevented pupils and teachers from travelling and damaged school heating systems and pipes.[10]

> A-level chaos as students fail to turn up for exams; tests go ahead despite thousands of pupils being stranded at home by snow.[11]

> We would expect head teachers to take a commonsense approach when deciding to close a school based purely on local conditions and the safety of children travelling to and from school.[12]

In the vast majority of places in the United Kingdom, schooling takes place as follows:

1. Primary school (Infant/Junior School) from 5 years old to 11 years old
2. Secondary school from 11 years old to 16 years old, at the end of which, pupils sit the national General Certificate of Secondary Education (GCSE) examinations. Pupils can choose whether to leave school at that point, or carry on for two more years for what is known as "6th form" education
3. 6th Form from 16 years old until 18 years old, in either a 6th form college or College of Further Education. Pupils will often take Advanced Level (A Level) examinations at the end of the 6th form. Some will then go on to university
4. University from 18 years old onwards (normally 3 years)

The 2010 big freeze resulted in widespread school closures, with ramifications across the whole service ecosystem. The ramifications are identified and discussed later in the chapter. At this stage, we highlight the key news items relating to primary and secondary schools.

As the third headline above implies, it is the final responsibility of the head teacher of a primary or secondary school as to whether or not to close the school. Where pipes are frozen or heating has failed, it is a relatively straightforward decision to close a school until the utilities are fully working. However, where it is a question of judging the safety of children travelling to and from the school, including safety of the playgrounds, it is a very difficult decision for a head teacher to make. Advice from the government's Education Secretary was only that decisions to close schools should be taken quickly, and made on a local basis! The evidence is that, in the 2010 big freeze, head teachers erred on the side of caution and chose to close schools if there was any possibility of incurring liabilities. School closures were much easier to operationalize than in previous big freezes, as parents could be reached and informed through text messages and e-mails. However, school closure decisions were questioned by commentators, and by parents who had to take time off work to look after their children during school hours. Parents, themselves, had difficult decisions to make. While the law does not set a minimum age at which children can be left alone, it is an offence to leave a child alone when doing so puts him or her at risk, and so commonsense and peer group pressure would mean that parents of children at primary (and possibly secondary) school age would have to make some arrangement for child care.

Health Services

Ambulances are responding only to emergencies where life is threatened, and routine hospital operations are being cancelled, in those health authorities that are snowbound. The freezing weather has caused an increase in the number of people with breathing difficulties or having had serious falls being admitted to hospital.[13]

To aid the Health Board, Local Authorities are providing drivers with 4x4s to make emergency deliveries to patients who need critical or emergency medication.[14]

The medical loan service gave out four times as many wheelchairs as normal as it was inundated with calls from people who have broken their hips, legs, and ankles on the ice.[15]

Winter in the United Kingdom always brings about an increase in deaths and illnesses. Around 25,000 more people die in the months December–March compared to other times of the year. In a big freeze, the increases are compounded by a number of factors:

1. Deaths and injuries in weather-related incidents—traffic accidents, falls
2. Elderly people suffering in sub-zero conditions
3. Large increases in demand for ambulance services
4. Depleted supplies of blood from donors
5. Difficulties in locating pharmacies that are able to stay open
6. Increase in flu-like illnesses
7. Increased risk of infection and heart attacks, as cold temperatures lower immunity and thicken the blood

In urban areas, only emergency treatments and calls for ambulance services were able to be provided. There were pleas for members of communities to make extra efforts to look out for, and look after elderly relatives and neighbors, and people with mobility difficulties. In rural areas, various volunteers, for example, St John Ambulance, Red Cross, and owners of four-wheel drive (4x4) cars offered help to reach isolated communities with essential services. It is a very different system of health service provision from that which operates in settled times.

Utility Services

Around 1,000 homes were left without power in the coldest temperatures recorded in the country after a flock of geese flew into an overhead power line.[16]

Arctic conditions could make the heating situation "very serious," with thousands of homes running out of oil. Energy Minister warned that oil supplies for heating would not be able to be delivered for three to four weeks.[17]

Lorries carrying 160,000 litres of bottled water were due to arrive in a bid to ease the plight of householders, many of whom have been without toilet and washing facilities since before Christmas, when temperatures were at their lowest in living memory.[18]

In 2010, domestic and commercial users of energy were dependent on supplies of electricity, gas, oil, and water, each of which can be cut off, or reduced significantly, through circumstances related to a big freeze. While several stories exist which highlight utility company employees working through the night in blizzard conditions to, for example, restore power lines, the overall picture is that these companies require help from volunteers and ordinary citizens to deal with ongoing energy problems. On the domestic front, it is elderly people who suffer most from energy deprivation and reductions, through lack of adequate heating. The charity, Age UK, for example, claims that, in winter, for every one degree drop in average temperature, there are around 8,000 extra deaths. Although, in the last 63 years, gas and oil have replaced coal as the major fuel sources, it is very noticeable that the stories of the effects of fuel shortages are very similar in 2010 to those in 1947 and 1962/3. It is as if no lessons have been learned.

Unsettled Times and Service

Unsettled times bring a different perspective to service, brought about through a temporary fall, for many citizens, below the level of consumption adequacy. Citizens, who in settled times are used to organizations seeking to offer service delight through the provision of a free amusebouche in a restaurant or an origami-inspired toilet roll in a hotel, find a totally different perspective on service delight. During a big freeze, service delight is characterized by being able to get out of the house, walking without falling, being able to get to shops to purchase basic foodstuff and necessities, and avoiding loss of pay for not getting to work. In these circumstances, service is seen as that which supports physiological, safety, and belonging needs, rather than the higher-order esteem and self-actualization needs.

Through examining the news stories above, together with many other similar stories, we have identified several aspects which emerge when citizens are temporarily disadvantaged. Many have come to light precisely because of the way citizens experience unsettled times. Nevertheless, the aspects uncover elements of the service ecosystem which exist in settled times, but which can remain latent, and so often ignored. Each aspect below will be discussed with evidence offered from the UK big freeze of 2010.

When citizens fall temporarily below the level of consumption adequacy:

1. their experiences are less dependent on organizational initiatives;
2. organizational value propositions are less relevant to them: citizens perceive that they are let down by many service providers;
3. well-being and quality of life depend more on citizen-to-citizen interactions;
4. *public* service has increasing importance
   a. citizens will contribute to co-production of public services;
   b. communities or individuals will "do it themselves";
5. there is a greater realization of networks, relationships, and interactions, and the implications of them—interconnectedness;
6. information and communication technology has a more prominent role in service and well-being;
7. they are forced to use and integrate their resources creatively.

We elaborate now on these aspects.

Citizen Responses

Under normal conditions, service provision is undertaken by organizations. In unsettled times, citizens can no longer depend on organizations providing the services. So service takes on a new meaning, and is often the result of citizens' own actions.

For example, the UK Meteorological Office (Met. Office), the organization responsible for providing weather forecasts, came in for much criticism for its failure to provide a comprehensive and up-to-date picture of snow and ice across the United Kingdom. This is despite its mission which states that through unrivaled know-how, it will enable individuals, society, and enterprises everywhere to make the most of the weather and the natural environment. A common complaint was that the snowfalls were much greater than the Met. Office forecast (sometimes 10 times as much) and that plans for dealing with transport problems were useless because they were based on poor weather forecasting advice. Indeed, many UK residents found the social network site "Twitter" more accurate than the official Met. Office forecasts, and a snow forecast website, UK Snow Map, was designed by an imaginative freelance web designer, using snow fall information from Twitter users in real time. It was based on reported snow fall amounts, rather than levels anticipated by the amount of cloud cover. Similarly, passenger charters from rail operators in which they aim to provide comprehensive, accurate, and timely train information, and mission statements from energy companies in which it is claimed that they will bring a sustainable energy solution home to everyone, are seen as irrelevant and unattainable in unsettled times. Local council propositions to create the best quality-of-life for its people are seen, in such times, as an unobtainable desire.

So what are the reactions of citizens to the inability of organizations to meet their aims, and continue normal service? Some take action and provide, for themselves, some of the services of which they are deprived. Some work and cooperate with formal organizations to co-produce mutual benefit. Some, on the other hand, voice their discontent to blame the formal organizations for not doing their best to rise to the challenges that the big freeze has brought about.

There are many examples of citizens getting together in communities to clear their own streets in the absence of gritting lorries. Bizarrely, though, the same group would be reluctant to clear the pavements (sidewalks) outside their individual houses. Such decisions were made on the understanding that if anyone was injured through falling in a wholly or partially cleared section of pavement, the person(s) who undertook the snow/ice clearing effort could be subject to litigation. Fellow citizens offered food and accommodation to those stranded in cars. Neighbors brought in food, warm clothes, and medicines to housebound, usually elderly, people. More reliable train information was supplied through citizens' use of Twitter. Owners of 4x4 cars responded to the plea to offer their services to take nurses to work. Charity workers launched a special helpline number for struggling farmers. Although formal organizations strived to produce their normal service, it was evident in countless examples that basic well-being of citizens depended on the actions and deeds of other citizens who engaged in volunteer activity for the general good of their local community. However, not all citizens' actions were altruistic. For example, communal roadside supplies of rock salt were looted to use on people's own properties, or to sell to other residents, and youths caused accidents through snowballing passing cars.

There are also many examples of citizens working side by side with organizations to meet challenges posed by the big freeze. Parents and pupils worked together with teachers to clear snow and ice from school playgrounds and pathways to bus stops. Volunteers pushed wheelie bins on behalf of elderly or infirm neighbors to points where refuse collection vehicles could reach. Mountain rescue volunteers worked with police and ambulance services to rescue people stranded in blizzard conditions. Temporary workers were recruited to help the Royal Mail with deliveries. Ambulance crews were assisted by members of the public to free vehicles stuck in the snow. On the advice of water authorities, volunteers checked homes, garages, outbuildings, and vacant commercial properties for frozen pipes and internal leakages. Citizens reported serious damages to road services to the highways department on a special helpline. Council staff and Red Cross volunteers worked together to provide food to isolated rural communities. In these instances, citizens recognized and accepted the limitations on the ability of organized services to fulfill their aims in the extreme conditions, and sought to use their own resources to assist.

Notwithstanding the citizen responses in the previous two paragraphs, there was considerable news footage of citizens attributing blame for their reduced well-being to various service organizations and their representatives. People were concerned that schools were being closed unnecessarily, and that refuse collectors were not making enough effort to negotiate side roads. Local councils and the UK government were blamed for lack of grit in many areas. Airports and airlines were heavily criticized for failures to put in place appropriate service recovery plans. Scorn was cast on the Met. Office forecast that the chances of a cold winter in 2010 were less than 15%, following a previous forecast that the rain-sodden summer would be an odds-on "barbecue summer." The Scottish transport minister was forced to quit over his handling of traffic issues in the big freeze—his lack of preparedness, and excuse of blaming the weather forecasters. The rail companies were heavily criticized for their lack of information to passengers stuck on trains and cold platforms. A parents' pressure group was formed in response to perceived poor handling of the A level examination situation as pupils were unable to sit examinations through weather-related delays. There was a widespread feeling that citizens had been let down by providers of services that contribute to their quality of life.

An Example of Interconnectedness—School Closures

Once pointed out, and evidenced through specific examples, many of the citizen responses above may be relatively unsurprising. What is less obvious is the interconnectedness between the elements of the service ecosystem, which remains latent until normal services are disrupted. Here we take one example, where a key feature of a community's service infrastructure—the school—is unable to function for a period of time, in order to illustrate the complexity of networks, relationships, and interactions that underpin citizens' place experiences. The networks, relationships, and interactions that emerge from news stories connected to school closures are presented in Figure 7.1, and will be explained in more detail. They are unlikely to be exhaustive as they rely on topics that newspapers feel worth reporting. Nevertheless, they identify "actors" in the education service system that are not immediately obvious but that are both responsible for, and affected by schools.

As may be expected, the main "actors" are the head teachers, the teachers and other employees, the parents, the children, and the various associated businesses. However, there are many other actors with influences on the service system: for example, utility companies; local authorities; lawyers; the Trade Union Council (TUC); the teachers' trade unions; parent organizations; employers (of the parents); government departments (especially education); Examination Boards and education quality watchdogs; and the Met. Office. All of the interactions depend to a large extent on the technological, social, and legal environment of the United Kingdom. Very much like a biological ecosystem, where the absence of a key species (e.g., Euglossine orchid bees which pollinate Brazil nut trees)

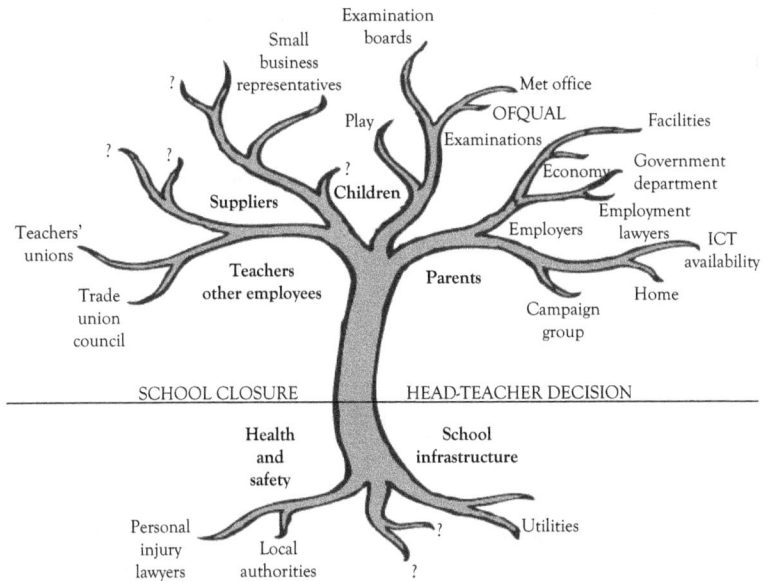

Figure 7.1. Actors and networks associated with school closures.

can have major implications for other species (e.g., Brazil nut trees themselves, the agouti that eats the Brazil tree nuts and scatters the seeds), the
absence of a key actor in a service ecosystem has major implications for
other actors. The failed attempts to grow Brazil nut trees in plantations,
away from the primary rainforest, demonstrated the complexity of the
ecosystem of which they are a part. Similarly, the unsettled times that
caused school closures, brings to light the service system complexities that
are not normally considered. We elaborate on some of them.

We start with the closure of primary or secondary schools at short
notice, based on the head teacher's judgment. There are many factors
which influence the decision to close a school, which we will examine
later. First, however, we look at the consequences of a school closure. The
most obvious consequence is that arrangements must be made to look
after school children during the school day. The school day varies between
schools, but is usually about 6–7 hours, starting at between 8.30 a.m. and
9.00 a.m. For many parents, this may involve one of them taking time
off work. So employers face a reduction of resources. When thousands
of schools close, this has a considerable economic effect, especially when
coupled with other employees not getting to work, or getting to work late

because of traffic and travel issues. Estimated costs of absenteeism were given for various regions in the United Kingdom: in Birmingham and West Midlands, £73 million per day; in Northern Ireland, £600 million per day; in Cardiff and West Glamorgan, £25 million per day.

Not all employers reacted in the same way. Some continued to pay the employees, recognizing in the main that the reason for not getting to work was not the employee's fault. There are examples of such employers seeking to enable employees to work at home or from flexible locations, which depended to a large extent on them possessing the ICT equipment to make this possible. Some would offer facilities which allowed parents to bring the children to the work location. Other employers, however, refused to pay employees who did not turn up for work. Those employees who were members turned to their trade unions for support. The Trade Union Council (TUC), the national trade union organization in the United Kingdom, representing the vast majority of organized workers who are members of trade unions, became involved and the issue became a national debate. Many employers and parents, at this time, began to question school closure decisions. The amount of absenteeism in the economy was blamed on what were perceived as unnecessary school closures. Teachers and head teachers were accused of not making enough effort to ensure that schools remained open. Teachers sought support from their own trade unions, and hence the TUC, as a further contribution to the national debate. Employment Law, and the rights of employers with regard to absent employees, became a "hot topic." Employers, government and the TUC all sought advice from the legal profession.

For many children, especially those aged 15–18 years, the big freeze in January and February 2010 came at a very inappropriate time—the sitting of elements of A Level and some GCSE examinations. The national examinations are set by Examination Boards, of which there are seven in the United Kingdom. Schools have the choice of any one of the Examination Boards on a subject-by-subject basis. The Examination Boards are all members of the Joint Council for Qualifications (JCQ) responsible for, amongst other things, information exchange between its members. The Office of Qualifications and Examinations Regulation (Ofqual) is the body that oversees the regulation of qualifications, examinations, and assessment in England. Ofqual maintained that tried and tested contingency plans were in place to deal with disruption to examinations and, together with statements from the JCQ and the UK government, sought to calm down parents and pupils who were concerned about the consequences of missed examinations through school closures, impassable roads, or both. However, the contingency plans did not anticipate multiple school or college closures, and the advice that alternative venues could be used proved to be unhelpful in the conditions brought about by the big freeze. Concerns that hundreds of thousands of pupils could be disadvantaged through missing examinations or having to take them in the following summer resulted in the formation of a Parents' Campaign group totally dissatisfied with the perceived inadequate responses from Ofqual and the JCQ, which simply advised those who were affected to contact the relevant awarding bodies (Examination Boards) and check their websites for guidance. As with other organizations, Ofqual laid much of the blame for the chaos on poor weather forecasts from the Met. Office.

A school closure affects many small businesses that depend on regular Monday to Friday activity. This is especially the case for the thousands of small retail businesses in the vicinity of schools for which a significant proportion of their takings rely on children's purchases before and after school and in the lunchtime period in many cases. Other businesses, for example, suppliers of school meals, also experience greatly reduced income during a prolonged school closure.

In examining interconnectedness between elements of the service system made transparent through school closures, it is instructive to explore the antecedents of the school closures. What must head teachers consider before making their decision? At the top of their agenda is the health and safety of the pupils (and the teachers and other employees). Access and transport to and from school are key to health and safety. Can a sufficient number of teachers make it in to provide appropriate supervision? Are the school grounds and approaches safe to walk on? In contrast to 1947 and 1962/3, UK schools and head teachers in 2010 live in an increasingly litigious society with personal injury lawyers overtly advertising their services and parental disputes with schools and teachers regularly receiving widespread news coverage. In these circumstances, head teachers are understandably reluctant to risk accidents where blame might be leveled at the school and, given the need for quick decisions, choose school closure as a precautionary measure. As was stated earlier, the mechanics and logistics of closing a school are made easier through the availability of e-mails and text messages to reach all the parents and other affected parties. Although school closures and their ramifications are brought about by the extreme weather conditions, they also reflect the technological, social, and legal environment that exists at the time.

In Figure 7.1, it is recognized, through the insertion of question marks, that not all actors/interactions have been identified through the news items accessed, and that the system features are likely to be even more complex.

Information and Communication Technology

Largely because of the speed of developments, especially with mobile technology, ICT played a major part in the responses of organizations and citizens to the abnormal weather conditions. It was the first UK big freeze in the era of social media. According to the Office of National Statistics,[19] in 2010, 30.1 million adults used the Internet every day or nearly every day, with only 9.2 million adults not using the Internet, and 73% of households had Internet access. Some 31 of Internet users connected via mobile phone. By February 2010, it was estimated that over 29 million people in the United Kingdom used social media sites, spending an average of 4.5 hours a month on them.[20] Organizations were learning how to use social media to reach large numbers of citizens with information on disruptions to travel, health, utility, public, and education services, with varying amounts of success. Conversely, the majority of citizens were able to "search the net" for information relevant to themselves, and use social media and blogs to voice their opinions and levels of (dis)satisfaction with service organizations. In a quirky way, however, some companies benefitted from a situation where many citizens were forced to remain at home with Internet access. See Figure 7.2.

Being able to use and benefit from the Internet in the many possible ways is a resource that citizens in earlier big freezes did not possess. This brings us to some initial thoughts on resources that citizens possess and use in the circumstances brought about by the extreme weather.

Snowed in Britons let their fantasies go wild and flock to extra-marital dating website

Britons snowed in by the wintry weather have been flocking to an extra-marital dating site in recent days.

IllicitEncounters.com, which provides a platform for married people to conduct affairs, says it has seen an unexpected increase in visitors over the past 24 hours and received a record number of new profiles overnight.

The website said most new members are registering from areas worst hit by this week's extreme weather, including Hampshire, Berkshire, and the West Country.

The site has hired several temporary staff to cope with the rush.

The Worst Snow in Decades is a Win for the Online Bingo Industry

The thousands of people snowed into their homes include many people playing bingo as a fun way to distract from the thought of venturing out into the wintry weather. As a result of the snowfall, many bingo operators have taken it upon themselves to offer special 'snowed in' offers, recognising the snow as a pretty good acquisition tool!

Figure 7.2. Opportunistic service provision.

Citizen Resources

It is only recently that detailed attention has been given to the resources that are used and integrated by citizens, customers, or consumers, either individually or in groups. Arnould, Price, and Malshe moved the focus from organizational resources to customer resources, and with an emphasis on consumer goals; life projects and life roles.[21] In the context of the SDL of marketing, they offer a framework—a resource-based view of the consumer—that details how consumers may use and integrate their oper-and resources (resources on which an operation or act is performed to produce an effect) and operant resources (the intangible resources that produce effects) in order to meet their goals. The operand resources consist of, for example, material objects (e.g., cars, computers, mobile (cell) phones) and physical spaces (e.g., houses). Consumers' operant resources are categorized as physical (energy, emotions), cultural (knowledge, skills, history, imagination), and social (family and commercial relationships, consumer tribes). Consumer/citizen goals in unsettled times tend to be shorter term, concentrating on surviving and coping. Nevertheless, responses to unsettled times and the temporary experiences of falling below the level of consumption adequacy highlight just how important citizens' resources, especially their operant resources, are in any service ecosystem.

It is not that they are unrecognized. However, normally they are labeled by phrases such as "community spirit" and "togetherness in adversity." The emphasis is on conveying a feel-good factor, rather on the greater enablement of citizen resources. The examples of citizens working together and with organizations to combat the unsettled times, chronicled above, suggest that citizen resources are crucial in these situations, and so deserve serious attention. We return to this theme in the next chapter.

The Next UK Big Freeze

When will it be? It could be next year. It could be 30 or more years away. What was the response to the 2010 big freeze, and what has been, and might be learned?

From the news stories, some strategies can be inferred about the efforts to deal with service supply under abnormal conditions during the 2010 big freeze:

1. Service prioritization and intensification
2. Service collaboration amongst organizations
3. Service cooperation and coordination
4. Service communication

Not all of them achieved the desired effects. Evidence shows that prioritization took place: for example, with the enormous efforts to salt/grid motorways and A roads, and dealing with emergency medical cases only. In the former case, it was arguably ineffective. Organizations collaborated to deal with issues as they emerged, for example, mountain rescue teams and ambulance services, and the sharing of rock salt between local authorities. The overall impression was that these collaborations emerged rather than were planned. The UK government was involved in several instances to coordinate resources, as, for example, road salting and education issues/disputes arose. However, often the governmental advice was no more than a suggestion that citizens should consult the appropriate website. Whilst recognized as very important, communication with the public was a major problem due to the sheer volume of demand. For example, at peak times, the National Rail Enquiry Service was receiving 1.5 million hits on its website in January 2010.

One UK governmental response was to recruit a team to review the resilience of England's *transport* system in winter, as part of a plan to cope with the next big freeze. Their remit was to focus on how to increase the probability of transport systems and weather forecasting systems operating more efficiently. Consequently, their report,[22] published in October 2010, covered operations of highway authorities, legalities of footways and self-help, salt utilization and supply chain, railways and aviation, and the economics of winter resilience. Many pages of the report deal with suggestions for technical improvements, for example, with the design of trains and snow ploughs, which would reduce disruptions. Also, there was an emphasis on improving communication with the public about the contingency plans for reduced services which have to be implemented by rail and aviation companies. The report estimated the economic and social costs associated with sub-optimal operations largely due to transport and travel disruptions, and posed the question as to whether it is even worthwhile increasing expenditure on winter resilience. Unfortunately for the transport winter resilience team, the second episode of the 2010 big freeze occurred only 1 month after the publication of their report, and before any recommendations could be implemented.

It is interesting that the government equated resilience to big freezes with resilience of the transport systems. Although the team considered the need for integration across transport modes, the full interconnectedness between all of the elements of the service ecosystem was not directly considered. It was not part of the remit. The focus was clearly, and understandably given the remit, on potential technical and logistical solutions to combat the effects of the big freeze. However, we feel that a focus on citizen well-being through service, employing ideas from service science, SDL, and transformative service research, could complement the existing focus on transport-related organizational responses to abnormal weather conditions.

Summary

The "big freeze" case study complements those in Chapter 5, and offers further insights through a more detailed evaluation of the effects of unsettled times on core service systems and their interconnectedness. The case study provides additional evidence of the desirability of a citizen-based focus on service in unsettled times. Therefore, we advocate that service research expertise should and could be used to provide a different lens through which to understand the effects of unsettled times. In the concluding chapter, using understanding obtained from the big freeze case study and the three case studies in Chapter 5, we:

1. put forward purposeful proposals for studies of service ecosystems in general, and for systems subject to unsettled times;
2. evaluate the robustness of service science, SDL, and transformative research frameworks to occasions when citizens fall temporarily below the level of consumption adequacy; and
3. make a plea for service systems expertise to contribute to policy-making with regard to large, long-term problems.

Review and Discussion Questions

1. Mobile technology enables urban system resilience. Discuss.
2. Explain how citizens use and integrate their physical, social, and cultural resources in unsettled times.
3. How can social media be enablers in unsettled times?
4. Detail the ways in which the core urban services of transport, health, education and utilities are interconnected. How might this information lead to strategies of system resilience?
5. Organizational value propositions are useless in unsettled times. Discuss.

CHAPTER 8

Bringing it Altogether

Purposeful Proposals, Challenges, and Directions

For many years we have engaged in research in marketing. As a consequence, we have, we believe, informed and intrigued many cohorts of students with the potential intellectual and practical challenges of marketing. Like many other scholars, however, we are aware of marketing's limitations. As Webster and Lusch maintain, "Marketing must be elevated to a higher level[1] of consciousness. A consciousness that grows beyond solving small, immediate problems, to addressing long-term, large problems that goes beyond individual customer satisfaction and short-term financial performance to encompass the total value creation system." This informed the aims of the book, stated in Chapter 1. It is our unease with the emphasis of much of current marketing research on "small" problems, coupled with the cynicism with which marketing is viewed by non-marketers, that has led us to pursue the issues contained in the aims.

The Focus of the Book

Elevating marketing to a higher level of consciousness can take many forms. We have focused on "service" and "unsettled times." Service(s) marketing has already made significant steps toward embracing longer-term and larger societal problems, as is evidenced through developments in service science, the service-dominant logic (SDL) of marketing, and transformative service research (TSR). However, there is, as yet, little evidence that it has directly and explicitly addressed issues faced by citizens below the level of consumption adequacy. Even the thought-provoking paper by Webster and Lusch, where they propose a shift from marketing's focus on customers "to a broader concern for *citizen-consumers*,"[2] relates largely to citizen consumers above the level of consumption adequacy; those who have the resources to make choices that go beyond simple survival.

Regarding the level of consumption adequacy, as described in Chapter 3, there are the majority of global citizens who are below the level of consumption adequacy (at the base of the pyramid), and those who are above the level of consumption adequacy (less than 30% of the world population). However, increasingly, there is evidence that citizens who are normally above the level of consumption adequacy can temporarily fall below it, because of what we have labeled as "unsettled times." The unsettled times can be brought about by climatic, environmental, economic, social, and political causes. There are also citizens who face the fall in level of consumption adequacy on a more permanent basis: vulnerable citizens who through illness, disability, or other chronic conditions lack resources to make choices that can improve their quality of life. The case studies in Chapters 5 and 7 provide evidence of experiences of citizens who fall below the level of consumption adequacy as a result of climatic and environmental disturbances, which can vary in terms of their impact (in functional, temporal, and spatial terms), and the likelihood with which they may occur (as discussed in Chapter 6).

Figure 8.1 demonstrates the focus of this book (shaded and in bold) within a larger framework based on the concept of consumption adequacy.

It is unlikely that there are greater, longer-term large problems for service marketers to address than those of the 70% of the world's citizens who lie below the level of consumption adequacy. However, as Martin and Hill[3] explain, research in countries where the majority of the citizens are at the base of the pyramid is particularly difficult to carry out. Even at the aggregate level, data on desired variables are measured differently or not at all. The marketing and consumer behavior literatures provide little or no guidance on how to gain greater understanding of societal consumption or impoverishment with regard to base-of-the-pyramid consumers. Research methods that are the mainstay of research on secure citizens above the level of consumption adequacy, for example, customer surveys

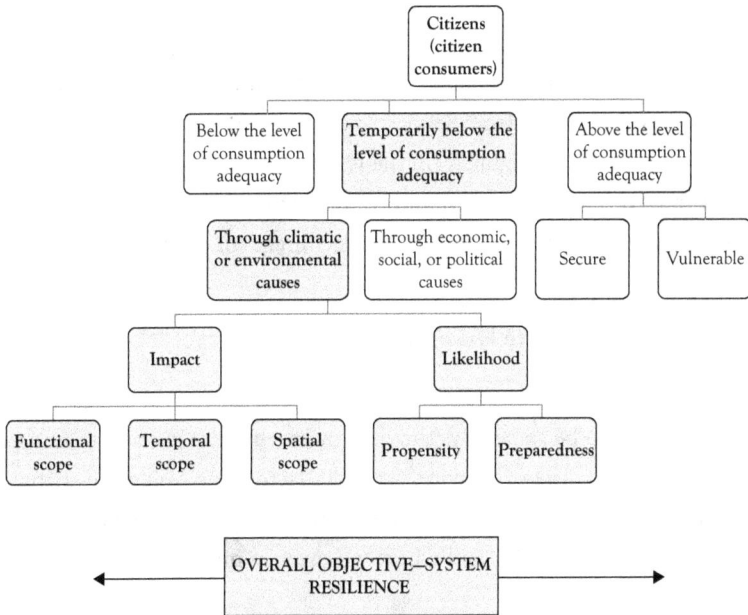

Figure 8.1. Citizens and consumption adequacy.

via questionnaire, are simply impractical, and inappropriate where survival is the prime aim in life.

All three authors went through the experience of the big freeze that was the subject of Chapter 7. While being in the relatively comfortable position of knowing that our fall in consumption adequacy was temporary, it opened our eyes to the service ecosystem of which we are a part, and provided the impetus for us to consider the lessons to be learned through service in unsettled times, especially in urban environments. It also alerted us to the strengths and possible shortcomings of current service marketing thought.

We recognize that the material in this book is a short step on a journey toward tackling the even larger problems. Nevertheless, the focus on service in unsettled times is original, and we hope that the insights (outlined below) will prove valuable to both practitioners and researchers. We echo the sentiments of Demirkan et al.[4] in their book on *Service System Implementation*, on the importance of starting "somewhere" in order to introduce new ideas and encourage advances in knowledge and understanding.

Purposeful Proposals

We start this concluding chapter by offering a number of purposeful proposals, based on ideas from service science, the SDL of marketing, and TSR, coupled with insights from the focus on service in unsettled times.

The set of purposeful proposals is summarized in Table 8.1. They represent suggested directions which will encourage innovation.

From Settled Times to Unsettled Times

The first purposeful proposal is concerned with the theme of the book: there is much to be gained by studying unsettled times in order to understand the real nature of "service," and the factors that underpin its provision. Such studies will tell us much about unsettled times, which is valuable in its own right, and which we cover in more detail later in this chapter.

An additional reason is that, through studies of service in unsettled times, latent features of the service system are uncovered that often remain unconsidered when times are settled. There are lessons to be learned from studying unsettled times even with respect to regions where the majority of citizens are normally living above the level of consumption adequacy. As Weinberger and Wallendorf observe, in unsettled times, "The taken-for-grantedness of norms disappears; people become more explicit and articulate about aspects of the meaning systems that previously organized

Table 8.1. Purposeful Proposals to Maintain Innovation

	Change Focus and Direction	
	From	To
1	Settled Times	Unsettled Times
2	Customer	Citizen
3	Customer Satisfaction	Citizen Well-being
4	Solving Immediate Problems	Understanding the Service Ecosystem
5	Business Resilience	Urban Service System Resilience
6	One-level views	Multi-level views
7	Consumer Attitudes and Behavior	Citizen Resource Use and Integration
8	Single Discipline	Cross-discipline

their behavior and beliefs. Focus is deeply concentrated on salient issues."[5]

From Customer to Citizen

Our second purposeful proposal is that a key change in mindset, that automatically broadens the scope of service marketing know-how, is required, which considers people as citizens rather than customers. Webster and Lusch's distinction is very useful here: "A customer is defined by its relationship with a seller; there can be no customer without a seller just as there can be no prey without a predator."[6] For people living below the level of consumption adequacy, permanently or temporarily, their lives and life satisfaction do not revolve around purchases from sellers, and they rarely play the customer role. In most cases, they are citizens, or citizen consumers. Citizens, whether below or above the level of consumption adequacy, fulfill many roles in their daily lives that do not qualify as the role of customer. Therefore, by taking a citizen perspective these other roles (family member, friend, neighbor, community activist) can be recognized as important contributions to a service ecosystem.

Another important feature of the world at the early part of the 21st century is that more and more of the world's citizens are living in urban environments. For example, in Beijing, it is estimated that some 7 million of its population of 19.6 million in 2010 are migrants from other parts of China, and that its population is increasing by an average of 600,000 people per year.[7] Mumbai's population has doubled from 1992–2012 to a metropolitan area population of 20.5 million, with a large majority of its citizens known to be migrants from other states of India.[8] The urban population in Brazil increased from 15.1 million in 2002 to 16.8 million in 2010 alone.[9] In Moscow, the flow of migrants from Russia and former Soviet Republics has led to an estimated population increase of between 1.5 million and 5.5 million, between 2002 and 2010.[10] This trend is not limited to the BRIC countries (Brazil, Russia, India, and China) which are seen as upcoming major economic powers. For example, in the United Kingdom, more than 80% of the population live in urban areas,[11] while in the United States of America the figure is 75%,[12] and in Japan it is 67%.[13]

It makes sense to focus on cities as service systems when addressing "large" problems. The effects of unsettled times, as illustrated in the cases in Chapters 5 and 7, are magnified in areas of dense population, demonstrating the need to learn more about the system of systems that make up a city.

From Customer Satisfaction to Citizen Well-Being

There has been a tradition in service(s) marketing to take the firm/organization perspective and seek to provide means for increasing customer satisfaction (or customer loyalty). The third purposeful proposal is that citizen well-being and quality of life (as per TSR) should supercede organizational improvements as the ultimate aim of service marketing research. While this is stated explicitly as one of the tenets of TSR, it is also implicit in the goals of service science where human problems are fundamental, and in those of the SDL of marketing where citizens are recognized as resource integrators in actor-to-actor co-creation activities.

It is also evident that citizen well-being is the motive behind many of the activities and interactions chronicled in the case studies in Chapters 5 and 7. As stated eloquently by one of the contributors to #quakebook, a compilation of first-hand stories about the 2011 Japanese tsunami:

> If Japan is to lift itself from disaster, enormous effort will have to be expended by a great many people. Tens of thousands are already working together under extreme pressure towards this goal, in the hardest hit Tohoku region, around the nuclear reactors in Fukushima, and throughout the nation and world. Millions have donated generously, and wish they could do more.[14]

From Solving Immediate Problems to Understanding the Service Ecosystem

Taking a city or geographical region as examples, it is clear that they constitute systems of service systems, where service systems can range from the individual citizen to the entire region. Any detailed evaluation of a region subjected to unsettled times through climatic or environmental disturbances (as illustrated through the case studies in this book), reveals very quickly the interconnectedness of the systems within the system: the service ecosystem. Knowledge of the interconnectedness is very limited, but it can be seen that service(s) marketing studies that fail to recognize the potential service ecosystem, and which focus on the small-scale, immediate problems that may exist between firms and customers, are at best limiting in their value and application. It also follows that research that involves data gathering and hypothesis testing may be premature.[15]

So our fourth purposeful proposal, which comes as no surprise to systems researchers, but which eludes most of the current practice in service marketing research, is that research should focus on gaining a greater understanding of service ecosystems. Although case study research can contribute to the understanding, there is scope for innovative research methods that capture the range of interactions, relationships, and emotions that make up service ecosystems. In unsettled times, and, indeed, in areas at the base of the pyramid, it is extremely difficult to gain first-hand knowledge of the workings of the service ecosystem by means of methods such as ethnography. This led us to take a second-hand, more indirect route in the case studies via newspaper reporting. We are aware, however, of autobiographical accounts of the effects of climatic and environmental disasters (e.g., Deraniyagala on the December 2004 tsunami in Sri Lanka,[16] and #quakebook on the 2011 tsunami in Japan[17]), which provide vivid personal stories of unsettled time traumas and the lasting effects. Research through storytelling may be a way forward, which can reach the emotional content of interactions that is only hinted at by newspaper stories.[18]

From Business Resilience to Urban Service System Resilience

In the well-established domain of crisis management, the notion of business continuity—"the process of planning to ensure that your business can return to "business as usual" as quickly and painlessly as possible in the event of a major disruption"[19]—has broadened into a study of business resilience. Business resilience is defined as "the ability of an organisation's business operations to rapidly adapt and respond to internal or external dynamic changes—opportunities, demands, disruptions or threats—and continue operations with limited impact to the business."[20] Resilience is spoken of in terms of businesses, and is limiting in scope in an urban context, especially in unsettled times, given that a business is one system in a system of systems.

The definition of urban service systems resilience, as the ability of assets, networks and systems to anticipate, absorb, adapt to and/or rapidly recover from a disruptive event (see Chapter 4), not only maintains the focus on citizens (not customers), as well as businesses and other systems within a service eco-system, but also has direct relevance to the case studies presented earlier in the book. The fifth purposeful proposal, therefore, is that urban service system resilience is a longer-term and more fundamental goal to pursue than business resilience. As the discussion in Chapter 6 suggests, research directed at how service systems can become more resilient to 'unsettled times' through the concepts of resistance, reliability, redundancy, and response and recovery (as discussed in Chapter 4) has promise in both academic and policy terms. This promise could be manifested in terms of informing the development of more robust systems that deflect the potential adverse consequences of unsettled times, and/or mitigate the impact of unsettled times when they do occur (through system design, preparedness and contingency planning, and so on).

From One-level Views to Multilevel Views

Many service marketing studies are currently located at one level—for example, employee-to-customer or business-to-business. Such studies may have limited systems impact. The focus on unsettled times brings out clearly the nested network aspects associated with systems resiliency. A resilient nation as a service system depends on resilient counties/provinces/states (as service systems) which, in turn, depend on resilient communities, families, and people service systems.

These levels of service system dependencies, which become very apparent through the case studies of unsettled times, are not necessarily given full attention during settled periods. A multi-level view of the service system ecology opens up opportunities for greater innovation and a move toward a higher level of consciousness.

From Consumer Attitudes and Behavior to Citizen Resource Use and Integration

The gathering of data on consumer wants, needs, perceptions, and motives, coupled with the aims of segmentation and positioning, that underpins much published consumer research, is undertaken on behalf of the producer, and is classified under the umbrella of business-to-consumer (B2C). Although it is justified through the term "consumer orientation," it is nevertheless a producer perspective, with consumers considered as relatively passive. This is in contrast to the mindset introduced through the SDL of marketing.

In developing the foundational premises of the SDL of Marketing, Lusch and Vargo[21] recognized the roles of *both consumers and firms as resource integrators*, following on from arguments presented by Arnould et al.[22] regarding a resource-based theory of the customer. As a result, FP9 was restated as "All social and economic actors are resource integrators." Largely, up until this point, the notion of consumers as resource integrators had attracted little academic or practitioner interest (in comparison to organizational resource-based studies). However, the increased recognition that consumers are regarded as more active, informed, and imaginative in the digital age, has led to early studies of consumer use and integration of resources.[23] In unsettled times, the case studies demonstrate many instances of how citizens use and integrate their operant and operand resources individually, in conjunction with other citizens, and with various organizations. Our sixth purposeful proposal, therefore is that attention of both academicians and practitioners should focus on what happens in practice—how citizens use and integrate resources.

From Single Discipline to Cross-Discipline

When IBM is recruiting people to engage with their service systems and service science research activities, they are looking for people they describe as T-shaped. T-shaped individuals have depth of knowledge in at least one system and one discipline (the vertical part of the T), but, importantly, must demonstrate breadth of knowledge and interest in many disciplines, many systems, and in boundary-crossing competencies (the horizontal part of the T).[24] These competencies include communication, networks, and organizational culture amongst others. Being expert in a single discipline is not regarded as sufficient to contribute significantly to the problems confronting service scientists. From an academic perspective, eminent marketing and service academicians argue that the elevation of service marketing to contribute to longer-term, larger problems will inevitably involve research that is cross-disciplinary and interdisciplinary.[25] So the final purposeful proposal is for discipline experts to move from addressing traditional and relatively safe topics at the core of their discipline to tackling less tangible problems at the fringes of the discipline, which entails moving beyond the discipline boundaries.

Once a discipline or sub-discipline matures, there is a natural tendency to define, often through academic journal objectives adhered to by successive journal editors, the boundaries of a discipline, and acceptable research within it. This can stifle originality relating to more innovative and unconventional research topics and methodological approaches. For example, services marketing research had, for many years, a focus on the provider–customer dyad, seen through the eyes of the organization. While this led to innovation in areas such as service quality and internal marketing (both organizational objectives), there was very little encouragement to pursue research into interactions beyond the provider–customer dyad (e.g., customer-to-customer) largely on the basis that they were outside the control of organizations. Through initiatives such as service science, SDL, and TSR, with their focus on the broader construct of service (rather than services), there is both a need and an encouragement to find out more about consumer-to-consumer, citizen-to-citizen, and actor-to-actor interactions, all of which are critical to 21st century issues, and which are central to service in unsettled times.

An area that we identify as particularly useful for cross-disciplinary research is the emotional effect on citizens of unsettled times; something which we see as an important area of study, but one on which our newspaper reports can only scratch the surface. The following extract from Deraniyagala provides a feel for the emotional impact of unsettled times on a citizen losing family members as a result of a tsunami:

> Half-drunk and half-drugged, I would search the Internet for images of the wave. Of scenes of destruction. Of dead bodies,

mortuaries, mass graves. The more horrifying, the better. I'd gape at these for hours. I wanted to make it all real now, but I had to be drunk to even try to do that. There was also a numbness in me, due not to drink but to a deeper deadness, that I thought was preventing me from being truly insane.[26]

In unsettled times, citizens experience transitions from settled to unsettled to being settled again (hopefully). Studies of emotions associated with liminal transitions such as these must call on many disciplines—for example, anthropology, sociology, psychology, geography, and health—as well as being part of consumer, tourism, and marketing research.[27]

All of the eight purposeful proposals are stated in the format "From A to B," but, to be absolutely clear, we are not suggesting the abandonment of any of the "A"s. The proposals are put forward to encourage both academicians and practitioners to take steps over to "B" as a means for generating novel insights into complex problems.

Evolving Service(s) Research and Directions

The evolutionary metaphor has been applied to give structure to the emergence of service(s) marketing and management in its early days. Fisk et al.[28] give a fascinating account of how pioneering researchers contributed to the evolution of a sub-discipline which provided insights into the now well-established areas of service quality, customer satisfaction, service encounters, service design, internal marketing, and relationship marketing. The evolution embraced the advent of e-services in the late 1990s, but, arguably, services research was reaching saturation in many of the above areas, with published research seemingly being judged as much by the statistical sophistication of the empirical studies as by the insights into service and marketing.

In the middle of the first decade of the 21st century, the time was ripe for "moving on." The impetus for the next stage in the evolution was provided by the three schools of thought: service science, SDL of marketing, and TSR. The moves from services (plural) to service (singular), and from organizational goals to citizen goals, are very significant, as we have emphasized throughout this book. In order to progress even further, we have argued that the notion of consumption adequacy could provide direction. Schools of thought should be evaluated not just against citizens who are above the level of consumption adequacy but also against citizens who are below the level of consumption adequacy, either permanently or temporarily (Figure 8.1). Truly unifying theories and frameworks should consider the majority of the world's citizens who are below the level of consumption adequacy.

Service Science and the SDL of marketing are very closely linked. As stated in Chapter 1, service science is supported by insights from the SDL of marketing. Therefore, we choose here to examine the foundational premises of the SDL of marketing (outlined in Chapter 2) as a means to assess whether adaptations to these schools of thought could/should be made in order to accommodate the challenges brought about through citizens being below the level of consumption adequacy.

Can the SDL of marketing move beyond the customer, as stated in FP6 and FP8, to the broader consideration of citizens, both below and above the level of consumption adequacy? There does not appear to be a reason why it should not. For example, in discussions of co-creation of value, there are arguments being put forward that value should be considered as "value-in-context," replacing the earlier notion that value is "value-in-use" as in FP6 and FP7. Value-in-use is based on the notion that value is co-created with *customers* and determined by them. Value-in-context emphasizes the importance of time and place dimensions and network relationships in the creation of value,[29] and has far greater resonance with the unsettled times considered in the earlier case studies. However, even in the helpful and contemporary arguments for moving the SDL toward "value-in-context" (e.g., Chandler and Vargo[30]), all illustrative examples assume that citizens live above the level of consumption adequacy. There is scope for coupling examples relating to citizens below the level of consumption adequacy with those above the level to provide greater support for the SDL as a unifying theory.

What about Transformative Service Research?

As indicated earlier, the focus of TSR is on service sectors and how they might be improved through adopting the goals of consumer well-being and quality of life. Berry and Bendapudi, for example, outline the challenges faced by the healthcare service sector.[29] However, the focus is clearly on the top-of-the-pyramid customers of healthcare. Even for these consumers, when unsettled times arise, as the case studies have shown, healthcare becomes even more complex as basic components such as ambulance services cannot be relied upon due to their interconnectedness with other service ecosystem elements. Taking a wider view of world citizenship, there is scope to assess the applicability of TSR to citizens permanently below the level of consumption adequacy. Basic health issues, such as household toilet facilities, require innovation coupled with intimate knowledge of systems affecting the lives of poorer or vulnerable citizens.[32]

Another service sector addressed currently by TSR is financial services. There are compelling reasons for studying this sector through a TSR lens, given the "financial crises" affecting many areas in the developing world in the late 20th century and then much of the developed world in the early decades of the 21st century, and the arguments to move beyond a predominantly economic approach to the problems with the sector.[33] In addition, there is much to be gained by examining financial services as they relate to citizens below the level of consumption adequacy. It would be interesting to study, for example, how banks can offer positive help to citizens in unsettled times, and whether their value propositions are still relevant in such circumstances. TSR research in cross-disciplinary studies can offer insights into banks' relationships with those citizens struggling to meet the level of consumption adequacy on a permanent basis. Bank loans, for example, have many potential consequences when made available to women in districts of rural India, all of which are related to citizen (and family) well-being.[34]

A TSR priority of reducing the disparities in well-being experienced by poor consumers and ethnic minorities, *through service entities*, may be somewhat limiting. It still feels like a producer approach to complex issues. Maybe the priority should focus more on the consumer or citizen entities and the macro environmental aspects (social; cultural; economic; technological) in order to be able to contribute to the well-being of citizens who are unable to meet the level of consumption adequacy for whatever reason.

Implications for Practice and Policy

Policy makers and service providers strive to increase resilience to unsettled times. However, unsettled times arise from a variety of different causes, and can have many consequences, depending upon a range of factors.

Classification of Unsettled Times

One way to tackle the complexity of unsettled times is to provide a classification of them that both practitioners and academicians should find helpful. Our attempt to do so has yielded the following (refer back to Figure 8.1):

1. Causes of unsettled times
   a. Climatic; environmental; social; economic; political
2. Features to be considered with unsettled times
   a. Relative impact
      i. functional scope
      ii. temporal scope
      iii. spatial scope
   b. Relative likelihood
      i. propensity
      ii. preparedness

We have argued that a focus on urban service system resilience would be particularly fruitful, given the worldwide trends toward urbanization, and the potentially greater devastation that results from unsettled times to citizens in cities or other densely populated regions. Our focus on climatic and environmental causes of unsettled times in no way belittles the importance of other causes, but those studies are beyond the scope of this book.

In terms of relative impact, we have seen through the case studies that functional scope—impact on the system of systems—can be seriously underestimated. There can be a tendency to identify a particular system, for example, transport, as a focus for attention as was the case with the

UK governmental response to the UK big freeze of 2010. This kind of reaction results in the equating of resilience with only resistance. Potential solutions are put forward which focus on technical improvements to, for example, trains and snow ploughs. While they are important considerations, they take a predominantly provider perspective and underplay the interconnectedness of systems within the service ecosystem. All the cases identify the importance of communication in unsettled times, and often it depends on mobile (cell) phones. From a citizen perspective, the principal technical improvement would be in longer-lasting cell-phone batteries. It is time that think tanks which are set up to improve resilience to unsettled times include a member with service science expertise, to complement the economists and service sector representatives.

In Chapter 6, the three case studies illustrated the potential differences in temporal scope of unsettled times. However, while the end points of the timelines represent a time when most provider services are back to normal, it does not necessarily represent the end of the effect of unsettled times on the affected citizens. In many ways, the unsettled times outlined above could be regarded by many that experience them as a liminal state. The concept of liminality refers to periods of change, where the usual hierarchies may be reversed or temporarily dissolved, traditions become uncertain, and future taken-for-granted outcomes thrown into doubt.[35] The duration of a liminal period may vary considerably, and moreover, the aftereffects on systems of unsettled times may linger long after the event causing them has passed. We have highlighted above the (often ongoing) emotional upheaval that is caused to citizens, and many remember vividly where they did and did not receive help from public and private service providers. For service providers, getting it right, through preparation for, and reaction to unsettled times, is an important aspect in the generation of citizen loyalty. Regarding spatial scope, even in cities and urban conurbations, areas/regions are often subject to several administrative, governmental, and jurisdictional boundaries which do complicate matters when unsettled times, brought about by climatic or environmental changes, occur. Snow, ice, floods, earthquakes, and waves know no boundaries. A major challenge in developing resistance in urban service systems is bringing together the many parties (stakeholders) to offer help that is most relevant to the citizens.[36] Refusing to share rock salt between local authorities, or only controlling floods within a certain delineated area, which does happen, is clearly counterproductive to overall resilience. It seems that state, federal, or national governments must react quickly to adjudicate on such issues/disputes, but, arguably are caught by surprise when they occur, if the UK big freezes are anything to go by.

This brings us to the issue of the relative likelihood of unsettled times, the propensity of such an event, and the preparedness of public and private service providers. Propensity and preparedness are very much linked. For example, an option for the UK government, regarding big freezes, is to risk being unprepared, thereby saving costly stockpiling of rock salt and improvements in rail infrastructure, based on assumptions that big freezes have occurred, and will continue to occur infrequently. However, such an approach may not be acceptable where the potential tragic consequences of not being prepared are much higher than a 2- or 3-month temporary fall below the level of consumption adequacy: for example, earthquakes in Japan. This raises issues about what constitutes an appropriate level of resilience so as to make optimal use of what might be very limited resources for cities, regions, and nations in an "age of austerity" where any expenditure of public financial resource is closely scrutinized as to whether it provides "value for money."

Citizen Resources and Roles

The citizen focus that we have adopted in this book, has alerted us most strongly to the need to fully understand how citizens use and integrate their resources, both in unsettled and settled times. Any service provider strategy should take explicit account of the ability and willingness of citizens to use their resources, especially those which fall under the heading of operant resources. In unsettled times, citizens' uses of resources become far clearer and are seen as integral to system resilience and effectiveness. This is also the case for citizens living permanently below the level of consumption adequacy. An illuminating example is shown by a group of the poorest citizens in Mozambique who have made a dilapidated, former hotel the home for 3500 people, with an elected mayor of the community and volunteers as security, and community officers.[37]

The operant resources used by citizens, and magnified when they are temporarily or permanently below the level of consumption adequacy, are physical (strength and emotions), cultural (knowledge, history, imagination), and social (networks, family, community). Together with access to information and communication technology (in many cases), citizen uses of their operant resources represent key inputs to urban systems which, arguably, are not fully considered in planning for resilience or future developments. The case studies provide many examples of citizens using their resources on an individual basis, or in conjunction with other citizens or organizations, to mitigate the worst effects of unsettled times. This raises the question for service providers as to how citizens' resources can be recognized and nurtured fully as integral components of urban system resilience, and to ensure that those same resources, if encouraged and recognized, are available in settled times as well. This is an important and major challenge especially for governments. It is recognized. For example, following the London Olympic Games in 2012, "feel-good" and community togetherness of citizens was seen as good for the UK economy, but difficult to measure or forecast. Togetherness does not happen only in adversity, but is probably best understood through stories by and about citizens in adversity/unsettled times.

Future Directions and Limitations

The unshaded sections in Figure 8.1 provide guidelines for future research and study. In the area on which we have chosen to focus—citizens temporarily below the level of consumption adequacy—we have selected the climatic and environmental causes to consider in this book. Research projects examining the other causes—economic, social, and political—will all provide rich qualitative data to enhance understanding. No doubt researchers will also face difficulties in accessing relevant and reliable data sources, but the challenges are well worth taking. We fully recognize the limitations associated with our chosen approach of case studies based on newspaper reports. We feel it has provided us with a reasonable sketch or outline of systems subject to unsettled times—sufficient to provide a preliminary classification and some purposeful proposals. It has also convinced us that the approaches offered through service science, SDL logic of marketing have relevance and promise for tackling some of the "larger" problems. Nevertheless, what is contained in this book should be seen as a springboard for further research and studies aimed at providing greater depth of understanding.

A much bigger and even more challenging field of research is that of citizens who are permanently below the level of consumption adequacy. It is reassuring that service researchers, as evidenced at leading service-related academic conferences, are engaging with studies of the base of the pyramid. Our overall impression, however, is that these studies are aimed at alerting the research community to this direction for research, rather than, as yet, providing depths of insight. Our hope is that cross-disciplinary and cross-cultural research developments will move this area forward.

As we know, in countries where the vast majority of citizens live above the level of consumption adequacy, there are still minorities who live below the level. In Figure 8.1, we have made a suggested split between secure and vulnerable to recognize this situation, assuming that vulnerable citizens are the minority who live below the level of consumption adequacy. However, even this understanding may be incomplete as this situation is really far more complex than this diagram is able to fully represent. Through our research we have begun to question whether in fact all citizens, wherever they are geographically based, may be vulnerable at some point in time. For instance, a citizen living above the level of consumption adequacy may experience a change in circumstances which negatively impacts upon their quality of life: a change in employment status, health status, or marital status for instance. The increasing number of citizens fleeing political turmoil and seeking asylum elsewhere presents an even more complex example of changing circumstances. Citizens in these circumstances may find themselves forced to leave a comfortable life with little notice, replacing it instead with a safe house equipped with only the very basic level of support.

Whilst the changes we suggest here may only be temporary and not on the scale of the unsettled times we have discussed in this book, they may nevertheless pose similar consequences to the individual citizen, in the worst case scenario resulting in them becoming homeless and destitute. Considering all citizens as potentially vulnerable is a line of thinking we have yet to see presented in the literature. We include it here as a line which opens up extensive research opportunities. Such opportunities include the need to understand more fully which factors are central to citizen security and which factors play a role in enabling the citizen to transition back to more secure circumstances. Is it due to having an extended support network? Or the provision of the State? What role does individual mental health and well-being play in this transition? And how can service systems be better able to support the needs of those in these circumstances? As with earlier suggestions, cross-disciplinary research is an important way forward in this area.

And, Finally...

We have been actively involved with service, marketing, tourism, and retail research and practice over several years. This book project, and the research and writing involved with it, has taken us well out of our comfort zone. It has been invigorating. We hope that the material in the book has encouraged you as students, academicians, business professionals, or all to step back and consider not only the challenges of understanding service as it applies to unsettled times, but also the insights that such studies may provide for service system improvements in general. We think that we have laid the foundations for novel directions for student dissertations, academic research, and business projects. If so, we have achieved our aims. We would very much like to engage in discussions with anyone interested in developing ideas put forward in the book.

Review and Discussion Questions

1. What innovative research methods could be adopted in order to gain a greater understanding of citizen experiences in unsettled times?
2. What roles do citizens fulfill which do not qualify as customer roles?
3. Outline the factors which contribute to greater urbanization in nations?
4. Define "value-in-context". Is it potentially more applicable to service in unsettled times than "value-in-use"? Why?
5. If a service science expert became a member of a 'think tank' on resilience to unsettled times brought about by climatic or environmental causes, what should be his/her major contribution?

Notes

Chapter 1

1. IFM and IBM (2008), p. 1.
2. Maglio and Spohrer (2008), p. 18.
3. Hastings (2012), p. 9.
4. Cabinet Office (2011), p. 14.
5. Baron et al. (2013) provide further details on the development of research into services marketing.
6. Chesbrough and Spohrer (2006).
7. Vargo and Lusch (2004).
8. Vargo and Lusch (2008), p. 6.
9. Martin and Hall (2012), p. 1158.

Chapter 2

1. Lusch and Spohrer (2012), p. 1491.
2. Maglio and Spohrer (2008).
3. Maglio and Spohrer (2008).
4. Maglio and Spohrer (2008), p. 18.
5. The *Service Science* website: http://servsci.journal.informs.org/
6. Spohrer (2010).
7. Dirks et al. (2010), p. 6.
8. Vargo and Akaka (2009), p. 32.
9. Vargo and Lusch (2006), p. 283.
10. Vargo (2011).
11. Vargo and Akaka (2009).
12. Constantin and Lusch (1994).
13. Vargo and Lusch (2008).
14. Vargo and Lusch (2008); Vargo and Akaka (2009).
15. Rosenbaum et al. (2011), p. 1.
16. Anderson et al. (2012), p. 2.
17. Anderson et al. (2012).
18. Oliver et al. (1997), p. 311.

19. Rust and Oliver (2000), p. 88.

20. Ostrom et al. (2010) and Anderson et al. (2012).

21. Lusch and Spohrer (2012), p. 1499.

Chapter 3

1. Prahalad (2010), p. 6.

2. Martin and Hill (2012), p. 1155.

3. Martin and Hill (2012), p. 1156.

4. Prahalad (2010), pp. 7–8.

5. Hill (2002), p. 20.

6. Martin and Hill (2012), p. 1158.

7. Nussbaum (2011), pp. 32–34.

8. Burdett and Rode (2011), p. 10.

9. Smith (2012), pp. 31–35.

10. Glaeser (2011), p. 70.

11. Burdett and Rode (2011), pp. 11–13; Davis (2006), pp. 22–26.

12. Davis (2006), pp. 22–23.

13. Burdett and Rode (2011), p. 11.

14. Turok (2009), pp. 13–14.

15. Musterd and Murie (2010), pp. 17–32.

16. Porter (1998), p. 78.

17. Although it is not without its critics, who would argue that, in order to get a fuller picture, specific clusters would need to be considered in a wider spatial context, and also that issues relating to the spatial scale of clusters need to be taken into account—Musterd and Murie (2010), pp. 23–24, discuss this in more detail.

18. Musterd and Murie (2010), p. 25.

19. Florida (2002), pp. 68–69.

20. Florida (2006), p. 29.

21. Florida (2002), pp. 215–218.

22. Glaeser (2011).

23. Gordon and Buck (2005), pp. 6–14.

24. UN-HABITAT (2008).

25. Gordon and Buck (2005), p. 6.

26. Santinha and Castro (2010), p. 79.

27. Santinha and Castro (2010), pp. 80–86.

28. Santinha and Castro (2010).

Chapter 4

1. Maglio and Spohrer (2008), p. 18.

2. IfM and IBM (2008), p. 1.

3. Turok (2009), p. 4.

4. Bitner (1992); Bitner (2000) and Sherry (1998).

5. Warnaby (2009), pp. 403–423.

6. Grönroos (2007).

7. Warnaby and Davies (1997).

8. Cresswell and Hoskins (2008), p. 394.

9. Getz (1993); Jansen-Verbeke (1986).

10. Aitken and Campelo (2011), p. 917.

11. Braun et al. (2010).

12. IfM and IBM (2008); Maglio and Spohrer (2008).

13. Ashworth (1993), pp. 643–649.

14. Lusch et al. (2010), p. 20.

15. Warnaby (2009).

16. Ashworth and Voogd (1990).

17. den Berg and Braun (1999), p. 995.

18. Chandler and Vargo (2011), p. 40.

19. Warnaby et al. (2002), pp. 877–904.

20. Maglio and Spohrer (2008), p. 19.

21. Corsico (1993), p. 79.

22. IfM and IBM (2008), p. 19.

23. Santinha and Castro (2010), pp. 82–88.

24. Dirks et al. (2010).

25. Santinha and Castro (2010), pp. 84–86.

26. IfM and IBM (2008), p. 18.

27. Dirks et al. (2010), p. 6.

28. Kotler et al. (1999), p. 137.

29. Short and Kim (1998), p. 65.

30. Gold (1994); Ward (1998), p. 182.

31. Rogerson (1999), p. 972.

32. Rogerson (1999), pp. 980–982.
33. Layard (2005).
34. Bowling (1995).
35. Nussbaum (2011).
36. Rogerson (1999), p. 982.
37. Cabinet Office (2011), p. 14.
38. Cabinet Office (2011), pp. 15–16.

Chapter 5

1. http://www.cred.be/
2. http://www.cred.be/
3. Dirks et al. (2010).
4. CIA (2013).
5. Rourke (2011).
6. Australian Bureau of Statistics (2013).
7. International cricket matches between England and Australia are referred to as the "Ashes" in recognition of the historical event when Australia first beat England and equipment was burnt as a result.
8. Mayes (2011).
9. Hume (2011).

Chapter 6

1. Ganeshan and Diamond (2009).
2. Turnbull (2011).
3. Watts (2011).

Chapter 7

1. For information, news items 1, 2, 9, 13, 14 relate to 1947; news items 5, 6, 10, 11, 15 relate to 1962/3; and news items 3, 4, 7, 8, 12 relate to 2010.
2. Dirks et al. (2010).
3. *The Guardian* (2010, January 7).
4. *The Northern Echo* (2010, December 2).

5. *Walesonline* (2010, December 17).

6. The Sun (2010, December 22).

7. *The Times* (2010, January 14).

8. *Daily News* (2010, January 25).

9. *Liverpool Echo* (2010, January 4).

10. *The Guardian* (2010, January 7).

11. *The Independent* (2010, January 12).

12. *Walesonline* (2010, January 13).

13. *The Guardian* (2010, January 7).

14. *Western Telegraph* (2010, January 11).

15. *The Sun* (2010, January 6).

16. *Chronicle Live* (2010, January 10).

17. *Daily Telegraph* (2010, December 16).

18. *Daily Express* (2010, December 30).

19. See Office for National Statistics, Statistical Bulletin, Internet Access 20-10, available at www.ons.gov.uk

20. www.clicky.co.uk/2010/02/social-media-statistics-february-2010, accessed 30/7/13.

21. Arnould, Price, and Malshe (2006).

22. http://webarchive.nationalarchives.gov.uk/20111014014059/ http://transportwinterresilience.independent.gov.uk/docs/final-report/wrr-final-report-2010-10-22.PDF, accessed 30/7/13.

Chapter 8

1. Webster and Lusch (2013), p. 389.

2. Webster and Lusch (2013), p. 390.

3. Martin and Hill (2012).

4. Demirkan et al. (2011).

5. Weinberger and Wallendorf (2012), p. 77.

6. Webster and Lusch (2013), p. 392.

7. http://english.peopledaily.com.cn/90001/98649/7372493.html

8. http://www.indiaonlinepages.com/population/mumbai-population.html

9. http://www.tradingeconomics.com/brazil/urban-population-wb-data.html

10. http://www.telegraph.co.uk/sponsored/rbth/society/8555676/Moscow-17-million-people.html

11. http://www.bbc.co.uk/learningzone/clips/a-history-of-urbanisation-in-britain/7811.html

12. http://www.wri.org/publication/content/8840

13. http://www.indexmundi.com/japan/urbanization.html

14. #quakebook (2011), p. 6.

15. Webster and Lusch (2013).

16. Deraniyagala (2013).

17. #quakebook (2011).

18. Readers are directed to Dawson et al. (2011) and Quinn and Patterson (2013).

19. http://www.londonprepared.gov.uk/downloads/businesscontinuity/makingplans/bcprehearsal.rtf

20. IBM (2004).

21. Lusch and Vargo (2006).

22. Arnould et al. (2006).

23. For example, Baron and Harris (2008); Baron and Warnaby (2011); Hibbert et al. (2012).

24. http://www.ceri.msu.edu/wp-content/uploads/2010/07/Tshaped-ProfImage.pdf

25. See Brown in Ostrom et al. (2010); Webster and Lusch (2013).

26. Deraniyagala (2013), p. 48.

27. See Gotham (2007); Kennet-Hensel et al. (2012).

28. Fisk et al. (1993).

29. Baron et al. (2013).

30. Chandler and Vargo (2011).

31. Berry and Bendapudi (2007).

32. For example, Gebauer (2012).

33. Gummesson (2009).

34. See Garikapati (2012).

35. See Horvath, Thomassen, and Wydra (2009) for a fuller discussion of the concept of liminality.

36. A promising approach is through the concepts of holistic service systems and whole service. See Spohrer et al. (2012).

37. http://www.bbc.co.uk/programmes/p00r97xc

References

Aitken, R., & Campelo, A. (2011). The 4Rs of place branding. *Journal of Marketing Management 27*(9–10), 913–933.

Anderson et al. (2012). Transformative service research: An agenda for the future. *Journal of Business Research*, in press, doi:10.1016/j.jbusres.2012.08.013.

Arnould, E. J., Price, L. L., & Malshe, A. (2006). Toward A Cultural Resource-Based Theory of The Customer. In R.F. Lusch., & S.L. Vargo (Eds.), *The service-dominant logic of marketing: Dialog, debate, and directions* (pp. 91–104). Armonk, NY: ME Sharpe.

Ashworth, G. (1993). Marketing of places: What are we doing?. In G. Ave., & F. Corsico (Eds.), *Urban marketing in Europe* (pp. 643–649). Turin, IT: Torino Incontra.

Ashworth G., & Voogd, H. (1990) *Selling the city*. London, GB: Belhaven.

Australian Bureau of Statistics. (2013). *Tourism Queensland: Tourism Facts and Figures*. Australia, AU: ABS.

Baron, S., & Harris K. (2008). Consumers as Resource Integrators. *Journal of Marketing Management 24*(1–2), 113–130.

Baron, S., & Warnaby, G. (2011). Individual customers' use and integration of resources: Empirical findings and organizational implications in the context of value co-creation. *Industrial Marketing Management 40*(2), 211–218.

Baron, S., Warnaby, G., & Hunter-Jones, P. (2013). Service(s) marketing research: Developments and directions. *International Journal of Management Reviews*, in press, DOI: 10.1111/ijmr.12014.

Berry, L.L., & Bendapudi, N. (2007). Health care: A fertile field for service research. *Journal of Service Research 10*(2), 111–122.

Bitner, M. J. (1992). Servicescapes: The impact of physical surroundings on customers and employees. *Journal of Marketing 56*(2), 57–71.

Bitner, M. J. (2000). The servicescape. In T. A. Swartz, & D. Iacobucci (Eds.), *Handbook of services marketing and management* (pp. 37–50). Los Angeles, CA: Sage.

Bowling, A. (1995). What things are important in peoples' lives? A survey of the public's judgements to inform scales of health related quality of life. *Social Science & Medicine 41*(10), 1447–1462.

Braun, E., Kavaratzis, M., & Zenker, S. (2010). My city – My brand: The role of residents in place branding. Paper presented at the 50th European regional science association congress, Joenkoeping, SE.

Burdett, R., & Rode, P. (2011). Living in an urban age. In R. Burdett, & D. Sudjic (Eds.), *Living in the endless city*. London, GB: Phaidon Press.

Cabinet Office (2011). *Keeping the country running: Natural hazards and infrastructure. A guide to improving the resilience of critical infrastructure and essential services.* London, GB: Cabinet Office.

Chandler, J. D., & Vargo, S. L. (2011). Contextualization and value-in-context: How context frames exchange. *Marketing Theory 11*(1), 35–49.

Chesbrough, H., & Spohrer, J. (2006). A research manifesto for services science. *Communications of the ACM 49*(7), 35–40.

CIA. (2013). *The world factbook.* from https://www.cia.gov.library/publications/the-world-factbook/geos/nz.html

Constantin, J.A., & Lusch, R.F. (1994). *Understanding resource management.* Burr Ridge, IL: Irwin Professional.

Corsico, F. (1993). Urban marketing, a tool for cities and business enterprises, a condition for property development, a challenge for urban planning. In G. Ave, & F. Corsico (Eds.), *Urban marketing in Europe* (pp. 75–88). Turin, IT: Torino Incontra.

Cresswell, T., & Hoskins, G. (2008). Place, persistence, and practice: evaluating historical significance at Angel Island, San Francisco, and Maxwell Street, Chicago'. *Annals of the Association of American Geographers 98*(2), 392–413.

Davis, M. (2006). *Planet of slums.* London, GB: Verso.

Dawson, P., Farmer, J., & Thomson, E (2011). The Power of Stories to Persuade: The Storying of Midwives and the Financial Narratives of Central Policy Makers. *Journal of Management and Organization 17*(2), 146–164.

Demirkan, H., Spohrer, J.C., & Krishna, V. (2011). *Service systems implementation.* New York, NY: Springer.

Deraniyagala, S. (2013). *Wave.* London, GB: Virago Press.

Dirks, S., Gurdgiev, C., & Keeling, M. (2010). *Smarter cities for smarter growth.* from IBM Institute for Business Value: http://ssm.com/abstract=2001907

Fisk, R.P., Brown, S.W., & Bitner, M.J. (1993). Tracking the Evolution of the Services Marketing Literature. *Journal of Retailing 69*(1), 61–103.

Florida, R. (2002). *The rise of the creative class...and how it's transforming work, leisure, community & everyday life.* New York, NY: Basic Books.

Florida, R. (2006). *Cites and the creative class.* New York and London: Routledge.

Ganeshan, S. & Diamond, W. (2009) *Forecasting the number of people affected annually by natural disasters up to 2015.* Great Britain, GB: Oxfam.

Garikapati, S. (2012). Microcredit and Womens' Empowerment: Through the lens of time-use data from rural India. *Development and Change 43*(3), 719–750.

Gebauer, H. (2012). *Innovation in developing companies.* Retrieved July 19 2013 from http://www.slideshare.net/hgebauer

Getz, D. (1993). Planning for tourism business districts. *Annals of Tourism Research 20*(3), 583–600.

Glaeser, E. (2011). *Triumph of the city: How urban spaces make us human.* Basingstoke and Oxford, US: MacMillan.

Gold, J. R. (1994). Locating the message: place promotion as image communication. In J. R. Gold, & S. V. Ward (Eds.), *Place promotion: The use of publicity and marketing to sell towns and regions* (pp. 19–37). Chichester, EN: John Wiley & Sons.

Gordon, I., & Buck, N. (2005). Introduction: cities in the new conventional wisdom. In N. Buck, I. Gordon, A. Harding, & I. Turok (Eds.), *Changing cities: Rethinking urban competitiveness, cohesion and governance* (pp. 1–21). Basingstoke, EN: Palgrave Macmillan.

Gotham K.F. (2007). (Re)Branding the big easy: Tourism rebuilding in post-katrina new orleans. *Urban Affairs Review 42*(6), 823–850.

Grönroos, C. (2007). *In search of a new logic for marketing: Foundations of contemporary theory.* Chichester, EN: John Wiley & Sons.

Gummesson, E. (2009). The global crisis and the marketing scholar. *Journal of Customer Behaviour, 8*(2), 119–135.

Hastings, R. (2012, December 6). Just two centimetres of snow causes transport chaos across UK. *The i Newspaper,* p.9.

Hibbert, S., Winklhofer, H., & Temerak, M.S. (2012). Customers as resource integrators: Toward a model of customer learning. *Journal of Service Research 15*(3), 247–261.

Hill, R. P. (2002). Compassionate love, agape and altruism: a new framework for understanding and supporting impoverished consumers, *Journal of Macromarketing 22*(1), 19–31.

Horvath, A., Thomassen, B., & Wydra, H. (2009). On liminality – Introduction to special issue on *Liminality and Cultures of Change. International Political Anthropology 2*(1), 3–5.

Hume, T. (2011, February 26). Mummy I got buried. Please make it quick. *The Independent.*

IBM (2004). Business resilience – the next step forward for business continuity. *IBM Corporation.*

IfM & IBM (2008). *Succeeding through service innovation: A service perspective for education research, business and government.* Cambridge, EN: University of Cambridge Institute for Manufacturing.

Jansen-Verbeke, M. (1986). Inner-city tourism: Resources, tourists and promoters. *Annals of Tourism Research 13*(1), 79–100.

Kennett-Hensel, P.A., Sneath, J.Z., & Lacey, R. (2012). Liminality and Consumption in the Aftermath of a Natural Disaster. *Journal of Consumer Marketing 29*(1), 52–63.

Kotler, P., Asplund, C., Rein, I., & Haider, D. (1999). *Marketing places Europe: Attracting investments, industries, and visitors to European cities, communities, regions and nations.* Harlow, EN : Financial Times Prentice Hall.

Kotler, P., Haider, D.H., & Rein, I. (1993). *Marketing places: Attracting investment, industry, and tourism to cities, states and nations,* New York, NY: The Free Press.

Layard, R. (2005). *Happiness: Lessons from a new science.* London, GB: Penguin Books.

Lusch, R.F., & Spohrer, J.C. (2012). Evolving service for a complex, resilient, and sustainable world. *Journal of Marketing Management 28*(13–14), 1491–1503.

Lusch, R.F., & Vargo, S.L. (2006). Service-dominant logic: reactions, reflections and refinements. *Marketing Theory 6*(3), 281–288.

Lusch, R. F., Vargo, S. L., & Tanniru, M. (2010). Service, value networks and learning. *Journal of the Academy of Marketing Science 38*(1), 19–31.

Maglio, P. P., & Spohrer, J. (2008). Fundamentals of service science. *Journal of the Academy of Marketing Science 36,* 18–20.

Martin, K.D., & Hill, R.P. (2012). Life-satisfaction, self-determination and consumption adequacy at the bottom of the pyramid. *Journal of Consumer Research 38*(6), 1155–1168.

Mayes, R. (2011, April 23). Experience I survived two earthquakes in two months. *The Guardian.*

Musterd, S., & Murie, A. (2010). *Making competitive cities.* Chichester, EN: Wiley-Blackwell.

Nussbaum, M .C. (2011). *Creating capabilities: The human development approach.* Cambridge, MA and London: The Belnap Press.

Oliver, R.L., Rust, R.T., & Varki, S. (1997). Customer delight: Foundations, findings and managerial insight. *Journal of Retailing 73*(3), 311–336.

Ostrom et al. (2010). Moving forward and making a difference: research priorities for the science of service. *Journal of Service Research 13*(1), 4–36.

Porter, M. E (1998). Clusters and competition: new agendas for companies, governments and institutions. In M. E. Porter (Ed.), *On competition* (pp. 197–287). Boston, MA: Harvard Business School Press.

Prahalad, C. K. (2010). *The fortune at the bottom of the pyramid: Eradicating poverty through profits* (Revised and Updated 5th Anniversary Edition). Upper Saddle River, NJ: Prentice Hall.

Quinn, L., & Patterson, A. (2013). Storying marketing research: The twisted tale of a consumer profiled. *Journal of Marketing Management 29*(5–6), pp. 720–733.

Rogerson, R.J. (1999). Quality of life and city competitiveness. *Urban Studies 36*(5–6), 969–985.

Rosenbaum et al. (2011). Conceptualization and aspirations of transformative service research. *Journal of Research for Consumers* (19), 1–6.

Rourke, A. (2011, January 2). Australian woman dies as Queensland floodwaters rise. *The Guardian.*

Rust, R.T., & Oliver, R.L. (2000). Should we delight the customer? *Journal of the Academy of Marketing Science 28*(1), 86–94.

Santinha, G., & Castro, E. A. (2010). Creating more intelligent cities: the role of ICT in promoting territorial governance, *Journal of Urban Technology 17*(2), 77–98.

Sherry, J. F. Jr. (1998). *Servicescapes: The Concept of place in contemporary markets.* Chicago, IL: American Marketing Association.

Short, J.R., & Kim, Y-H. (1998). Urban crises/urban representations: selling the city in difficult times. In T. Hall & P. Hubbard (Eds.), *The entrepreneurial city: Geographies of politics, regimes and representations* (pp. 55–75). Chichester, EN: John Wiley & Sons.

Smith, L. (2012). *The new north: The world in 2050.* London, GB: Profile Books.

Spohrer, J. C. (2010). Service Science: Progress and directions. AMA SERVSIG, Porto Portugal at FEUP engineering school. June 2010.

Spohrer, J., Piciocchi, P. & Bassano, C. (2012). Three frameworks for service research: exploring multilevel governance in nested, networked systems. *Service Science 4*(2), 147-160.

Thequakebook community. (2011) *2:46: Aftershocks: Stories from the Japan earthquake.* London, GB: Kindle Edition.

Turnbull, M. (2011, January 12). It's 2011 and we've never been so vulnerable. *The Times.*

Turok, I. (2009). The distinctive city: pitfalls in the pursuit of differential advantage. *Environment and Planning A 41*(1), 13–30.

UN HABITAT (2008). *State of the world's cities report2008/09: Harmonious cities.* London, GB: Earthscan.

Van den Berg, L., & Braun, E. (1999). Urban competitiveness, marketing and the need for organising capacity. *Urban Studies 36*(5–6), 987–999.

Vargo, S.L., & Akaka, M.A. (2009). Service-Dominant Logic as a Foundation for Service Science: Clarifications. *Service Science 1*(1), 32–41.

Vargo, S. L. (2011). Market systems, stakeholders and value propositions: Toward a service-dominant logic-based theory of the market. *European Journal of Marketing 45*(1), 217–222.

Vargo, S. L., & Lusch, R. F. (2004). Evolving to a new dominant logic for marketing. *Journal of Marketing 68*(1), 1–17.

Vargo, S. L, & Lusch, R. F. (2006). Service-dominant logic: reactions, reflections and refinements. *Marketing Theory 6*(3), 281-288.

Vargo, S. L, & Lusch, R. F. (2008). Service-dominant logic: Continuing the evolution. *Journal of the Academy of Marketing Science 36*(1), 1–10.

Ward, S.V. (1998). *Selling places: The marketing and promotion of towns and cities 1850-2000,* London, GB: E. & F.N. Spon.

Warnaby, G. (2009). Towards a service-dominant place marketing logic. *Marketing Theory 9*(4), 403–423.

Warnaby, G., & Davies, B. J. (1997). Commentary: Cities as service factories? Using the servuction system for marketing cities as shopping destinations. *International Journal of Retail & Distribution Management 25*(6), 204–210.

Warnaby, G., Bennison, D., Davies, B.J., & Hughes, H. (2002). Marketing UK towns and cities as shopping destinations. *Journal of Marketing Management 18*(9/10), 877–904.

Watts, J. (2011, April 2). Weekend: Natural disasters: Japan earthquake. *The Guardian.*

Webster, F.E. Jr., & Lusch, R.F. (2013). Elevating marketing: Marketing is dead! long live marketing!. *Journal of the Academy of Marketing Science 41*, 389–399.

Weinberger, M.F., & Wallendorf, M. (2012). Intracommunity gifting at the intersection of contemporary moral and market economies. *Journal of Consumer Research 39*(1), 74–92.

Index

OTHER TITLES IN OUR SERVICE SYSTEMS AND INNOVATIONS IN BUSINESS AND SOCIETY COLLECTION

Jim Spohrer, IBM and Haluk Demirkan, Arizona State University, Collection Editors

- *Lean Sigma Methods and Tools for Service Organizations: The Story of a Cruise Line Transformation* by Jaideep Motwani, Rob Ptacek, and Richard Fleming
- *Business Engineering and Service Design with Applications for Health Care Institutions* by Oscar Barros
- *Designing Service Processes to Unlock Value* by Joy Field

FORTHCOMING IN THIS COLLECTION

- *Service Thinking: The Seven Principles to Discover Innovative Opportunities 12/15/2013* by Hunter Hastings and Jeff Saperstein
- *Service Mining: Framework and Application 12/31/2013* by Wei Lun ("Allen") Chang
- *Discovering the Service Imperative: How Understanding Your Customers Can Save Your Business 1/31/2014* by Douglas Morse and Haluk Demirkan
- *Service Design: A Collaborative Approach 4/15/2014* by Lia Patricio, Raymond Fisk, and Birgit Mager
- *Moving from Products to Services: Transformative Changes to Achieve Success 8/15/2014* by Valarie A. Zeithaml, Stephen W. Brown, and Mary Jo Bitner
- *Lean Management in Higher Education: The Transformation of Processes and Services at Fisk University 8/15/2014* by H. James Williams, Jaideep Motwani, and Rob Ptacek

Announcing the Business Expert Press Digital Library

Concise E-books Business Students Need
for Classroom and Research

This book can also be purchased in an e-book collection by your library as
- a one-time purchase,
- that is owned forever,
- allows for simultaneous readers,
- has no restrictions on printing, and
- can be downloaded as PDFs from within the library community.

Our digital library collections are a great solution to beat the rising cost of textbooks. e-books can be loaded into their course management systems or onto student's e-book readers.

The **Business Expert Press** digital libraries are very affordable, with no obligation to buy in future years. For more information, please visit **www.businessexpertpress.com/librarians**. To set up a trial in the United States, please contact **Adam Chesler** at *adam.chesler@ businessexpertpress.com* for all other regions, contact **Nicole Lee** at *nicole.lee@igroupnet.com*.

www.ingramcontent.com/pod-product-compliance
Lightning Source LLC
Chambersburg PA
CBHW070921270326
41927CB00011B/2668